Penguin Handbooks

Type It Yourself

Brenda Rowe took a secretarial course after graduating, and then
entered publishing. She is a publisher, and also writes as a
freelance. She lives in the middle of London, within walking
distance of her office. Apart from her work, her hobbies are family
and local histories, exchanging puns with her friends, and procras-
tinating. Her chief ambition is to write a really good novel – but
she continually postpones actually putting pen to paper.

Brenda Rowe

Type It Yourself

Penguin Books

PENGUIN BOOKS

Published by the Penguin Group
27 Wrights Lane, London W8 5TZ, England
Viking Penguin Inc., 40 West 23rd Street, New York, New York 10010, USA
Penguin Books Australia Ltd, Ringwood, Victoria, Australia
Penguin Books Canada Ltd, 2801 John Street, Markham, Ontario, Canada L3R 1B4
Penguin Books (NZ) Ltd, 182–190 Wairau Road, Auckland 10, New Zealand

Penguin Books Ltd, Registered Offices: Harmondsworth, Middlesex, England

First published by Pitman Publishing 1975
Published in Penguin Books 1981
10 9 8 7 6

Made and printed in Great Britain by
BPCC Hazell Books
Aylesbury, Bucks, England
Member of BPCC Ltd.
Phototypeset in Great Britain by
Filmtype Services Limited, Scarborough

Contents

Contents

Why learn to type?

Many people own a portable typewriter or have the use of a typewriter. But they don't make the best use of it because they haven't learnt to type properly. This book is for them.

It's for anyone who wants to learn the skill of typewriting and who is willing to spend a little time acquiring that skill. It isn't difficult to learn to type as long as you're prepared to practise.

In *Type It Yourself* the business of learning has been made as easy as possible. The book is divided into small units so that you don't have to learn a lot at once. And the order in which you're taught (although it may *look* haphazard!) has been worked out scientifically: partly to help you avoid the beginner's tendency to confuse left-hand and right-hand keys; and partly to teach you to type the more common letters first. The book has been designed, too, to make work as easy as possible for you – with a different typeface to draw your attention to new letters.

If you work through this book, your typing will no longer be a two-finger chore. It will be a skill – and, I hope, a pleasure.

Brenda Rowe

Unit 1   Before you begin

Before you start to teach yourself to type, you need certain pieces of equipment. Most of them are very simple; but you'll find typing easier if you take a little trouble at the beginning to make yourself comfortable.

Your desk

You don't need a proper desk. In fact, some desks are completely unsuitable for typing because they are not firm enough. Look around where you live to find a strong table that won't shake when you begin to type fast. A kitchen table is often satisfactory. The position of the legs should be such that you can sit right up to the table. The table should be in a good light so that you can read without straining, and without having to bend to read anything placed at the side of your typewriter.

Your chair

A straight-backed dining-room chair is often the best. The height recommended by the experts is from $15\frac{1}{2}$ inches to $19\frac{1}{2}$ inches (393 mm to 494 mm), depending on how tall you are. If you are going to be comfortable while you are typing, your thighs should be roughly parallel with the floor. When you put your fingers on the keys (the levers at the front of the machine on which the characters are printed), your hands should be parallel with the slope of the keyboard.

If you can't find a table and chair of the right height, use cushions to make the chair higher, or telephone directories to make the table higher.

Your typewriting mat

You may not think that a mat under your typewriter is necessary. When you work up a speed, though, the right sort of mat helps to stop your typewriter from shifting across the table. It also makes typing much less noisy, which is an advantage – for your family and neighbours, at any rate!

A mat needn't be one specially designed for the purpose. It can be a rubber car mat; or a 36-inch square sample of foam-backed carpet; or a square of thin foam rubber. The chief thing to remember is that it must be big enough for the whole of your typewriter to stand on. It must also have a non-slip base.

The paper you use

Don't try to learn to type on odd scraps of paper. What you type won't look nice, and you'll waste a lot of time looking round for pieces of paper when you should be practising. Buy yourself a packet of thick white paper. The best size is A4 (8¼ inches by 11¾ inches, or 210 mm by 297 mm). The exercises in the early part of this book are suitable for this size of paper.

Also find or buy a file or folder to keep your exercises in when you've finished typing them.

Your typewriter

There are many different makes of typewriter. They have the same basic arrangement so far as the letters of the alphabet are concerned; but some of the gadgets on the typewriter are in different places. You'll be told when to look out for these differences.

An important difference to look out for right at the beginning is whether your typewriter is a manual or electric one. This book is intended to be used with a manual typewriter. If you want to learn to type on an electric machine, you need a different touch. You don't need to *strike* the keys: all you have to do is to touch them, and they will automatically type.

Where to put everything

Your typewriter should be on its mat, with the front of the machine flush with the edge of your table. Your book can be on either the left-hand or the right-hand side of your typewriter, whichever suits your vision better. If you find that you have any difficulty in keeping the book flat when it's open, use a bulldog clip or a springtop spectacle case to weight down one side.

When to practise

It's a good idea to think now about when you're going to practise. The time of day doesn't matter; but if you have a routine you're much more likely to practise *daily*. And you'll learn to type much more quickly if you practise for a little while every day rather than for two hours once a week.

Even if you can already type with two fingers, don't skip any of the exercises. Work steadily through them, following the instructions.

While you're learning, don't try to combine two-finger typing with the method taught in this book (if you *have* to type a letter, go back temporarily to your old-fashioned two-finger method). When you're using this book, use the method shown here. But once you've learnt the whole of the keyboard from the book, stick to this method, and give up using only two fingers. It may make you type slighly more slowly for a little while; but, when you've got used to using all your fingers, you'll be able to type much more quickly.

Unit 2   Finding your way round your typewriter

On the top of your typewriter you will see a **roller**. Behind it is a **scale**. The markings on the scale are equal to the width of one letter on your typewriter.

At the left-hand side of the scale there is the **paper guide**. It can be moved along the scale in either direction. Usually, it is placed at **0** on the scale. Its functions are to help you put the paper into your typewriter at the right place, and to help you put it in straight.

The **margin stops** on your typewriter are to help you to keep the margins straight. For most exercises in the earlier part of this book you need margins of **30** at the left-hand side and **80** on the right-hand side. Find out where the margin stops are on your machine. Usually, they are levers that move along the scale: one for the left-hand margin, and one for the right. Move them along to **30** and **80** respectively, so that you are ready to start typing your first exercise.

Next, you need to fix the **line-spacing** – that is, the space between lines of typewriting. There's a lever for this. Find out where it is on your typewriter. Usually it's by the left-hand end of the roller. It's marked either:

$$
\begin{array}{ccc}
1 & & \dfrac{1}{} \\[6pt]
2 & \text{or} & \dfrac{2}{} \\[6pt]
3 & & 3
\end{array}
$$

For most of the exercises, you should set it at **1**.

So, before you start:

paper guide at 0
margin stops at **30** and **80**
line-space indicator at **1**

Now take a sheet of paper by its long edge, in your left hand. Drop it behind the roller with its left-hand edge against the paper guide. Turn the knob at the right-hand end of the roller away from you. The paper should appear at the front of the roller. Go on turning the knob until there's about an inch of paper showing at the front.

If the paper is crooked, use the **paper-release lever**. This is at the right-hand side of most typewriters, behind the roller. Pull it forward. Then you will find that you can straighten the paper easily. Move the lever back once the paper is straight.

Now find the **carriage-return lever**. This is fixed to the left-hand end of the roller, and is usually jutting forwards. With the palm downwards, raise your left hand and with a quick firm movement strike the carriage-return lever as far as you can to the right. Now you are ready to start typing. Look at this keyboard chart:

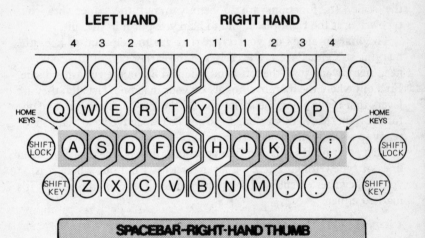

The characters shaded in are the ones you are going to type first – **asdf;lkj**. When you start typing, you'll be typing small letters. You'll learn how to type capital letters later on.

Look at the keyboard of your typewriter. Put:

the little finger of your left hand on **A**

the third finger of your left hand on **S**
the second finger of your left hand on **D**
the first finger of your left hand on **F**

Now put the fingers of your right hand in position:

the little finger goes on **;**
the third finger goes on **L**
the second finger goes on **K**
the first finger goes on **J**

With a sure firm touch push down the little finger of your left hand. Directly you have pushed the key down, release your finger. Now do the same with the third finger of your left hand.

(Are the fingers of your right hand still in place? They should be – the whole basis of typing-without-looking is keeping your fingers in position over these **home keys**.)

Now strike with the second finger of your left hand, and then with the first.

Do the same with the fingers of your right hand. Then look at the paper in your typewriter. You should have typed this:

asdf;lkj

But don't worry about what you are typing at present. Just get used to the movement of the keys and to keeping your fingers on these home keys.

Practise striking each key in turn again; and again. See how fast you can go just striking each one in turn. Return the carriage by using the **carriage-return lever**.

Take your eyes off the keyboard, and type the eight keys again without looking. Return the carriage and type them again. If you feel your fingers are still a bit stiff, go on practising like this. Even if you learn to type at a hundred words a minute, you'll still be using the same fingers on the same keys as you are now.

When you've finished, take the paper out of the typewriter. To do this, pull the **paper-release lever** forward. Then pull the paper out from the front with your left hand. Mark it with the date. Put the sheet of paper in your file.

Before you pack up for the day, check that you know where these gadgets are:

the paper guide
the line-space lever
the paper-release lever

If you're not sure, read this unit again.

Unit 3   The letters **a** and **l**

Move the paper-release lever back (you've left it up from your last unit). Then take a sheet of paper by its long edge in your left hand. Drop it behind the roller with its left-hand edge against the paper guide. Turn the knob at the right-hand end of the roller away from you. The paper should appear at the front of the roller. Move the knob until there's about an inch of paper showing. If the paper is crooked, use the paper-release lever and straighten the paper.

Check your margin stops – they should still be at 30 and 80. Strike the carriage-return lever with your left hand so that you are ready to start typing at the left-hand margin point.

Put your fingers on the home keys. Type each of the home keys in turn, beginning with the little finger of your left hand. Do this twice, then strike the carriage-return lever, and type the home keys three more times. If you feel you'd still like to "warm up", type another row.

Look at the chart:

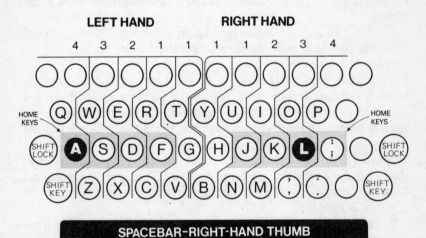

The keys with the white letters are the ones you're going to type. This time you're going to learn to type them without looking at your typewriter. You type **a** with the little finger of your left hand, and **l** with the third finger of your right hand. Put your fingers on the home keys. Look away from the typewriter and look at this book. Type:

allaalla

In the next exercise you have to leave spaces between letters. The **spacebar** is a long bar below all the other keys. You tap it with your right thumb to make a space. Practise doing this, leaving the fingers on their home keys.

Return the carriage and type:

a all alla la ala lal a all alla la ala lal a

Return the carriage and type:

lal alla a all lalla ala lal alla a all lalla

Keep your eyes on the book. Return the carriage. Type:

al a lal all ala a all al a lal all ala a all

Are you remembering to tap the spacebar? Now type:

a all alla la ala lal a all alla la ala lal

(carriage return)

lal alla all lalla ala lal alla all lalla ala

(carriage return)

al a lal all ala a all al a lal all ala a all

You should now be able to type these two letters quickly and without hesitation.

Take the paper out of your typewriter, by moving the paper-release lever forwards. Then pull the paper out from the front with your left hand. Mark the sheet of paper with the date, and put it in your file.

Unit 4 The letter **d**

Insert the paper. You should now be able to do this automatically, holding the long edge of the paper in your left hand, and using the knob at the right-hand end of the roller. If you're not getting it in straight, practise several times.

Check the margin stops. Use the carriage-return lever to move the carriage back to the left-hand margin.

As a warming-up exercise, put your fingers on their home keys and strike each key in turn, starting with the little finger of your left hand. Repeat this twice. Return the carriage.

Now type the following as fast as you can:

a all alla la ala lal a all alla la ala lal a

Now type:

lal alla a all lalla ala lal alla a all lalla

If you are hesitating over this exercise, type it once more.

Look at the chart:

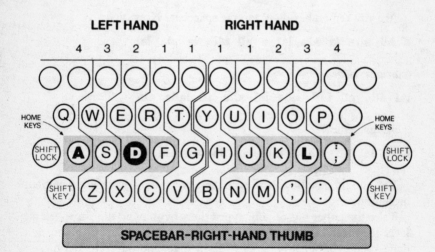

You are now going to learn to type the letter **d**. This is another of the home keys. You type it with the second finger of your left hand. Practise striking it several times. Now strike the carriage-return lever, and type the following:

a **d** l a**dd** la**d** all **d**a**d** a **d** l a**dd** la**d** all **d**a**d**

(*carriage return*)

alla **d**all **d**al **d**all lal**d** alla **d**all **d**al**d** **d**all

(*carriage return*)

a **d** l a**dd** la**d** all **d**a**d** a**dd** l a**dd** la**d** all **d**a**d**

Are you keeping your eyes on this book? If you're not, type the last line again, concentrating on what you're copying.

Take the paper out of your typewriter. Mark the sheet with the date and put it in your folder.

Unit 5   The letter **o**

Insert the paper. Put your fingers on their home keys. Practise typing **d** several times. Now practise your home keys exercise, striking each key in turn quickly and firmly, beginning with the little finger of your left hand.

Now type:

a **d** l a**dd** la**d** all **d**a**d** a **d** l a**dd** la**d** all **d**a**d**

(*carriage return*)

alla **d**all **d**al**d** **d**all lal**d** alla **d**all **d**al**d** **d**all

Now type:

a d l ada lad all dad a d l add lad all dad

Look at the last line you've typed. Look back at the book. Check letter for letter. Mark in pencil in a circle in the margin the number of errors. Put a tick in the margin if it's all correct. You should now be able to type this exercise with at most one mistake. If you have made more, type the line again.

Look at the chart:

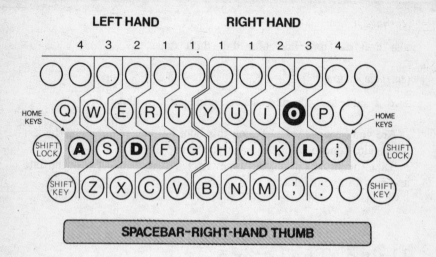

The new letter for you to learn is **o**. To type it you use the third finger of your right hand. Put *all* your fingers back on their home keys. Type **l**. Now move the third finger of your right hand upwards and slightly to the left and strike **o**. With all your other fingers still on their home keys type:

l**o** l**o** ll **o**l l**o**l **oo** l**o** l**o** ll **o**l l**o**l **oo** l**o** l**o**

(carriage return)

Now type the following, returning the carriage at the end of each line. You won't be reminded to do this any more.

a l **o** d al a**o** ad a l **o** d al a**o** ad a l **o** d
la l**o** ld da d**o** dl **o**ll**o** **o**ld**o** alla ald**o**
all **o**ld lad dad ad**o** add **o**dd **o**ld lad dad
l**o**ad d**o**ll dada l**o**ll l**o**ad d**o**ll dada l**o**ll

How quickly are you returning the carriage?

Type these words, returning the carriage after each one, and returning the fingers of your left hand to their home keys without looking at the keyboard:

all
old
dad
all
old
dad

Take the paper out of the typewriter, date it, and put it in your folder. Do this at the end of each unit.

Unit 6 The letter e

Insert the paper into your typewriter. Practise several times typing the letter o, returning the third finger of your right hand to its home key l after each typing. Keep your other fingers on their home keys.

Type the following. Return the carriage at the end of each line.

a load a doll a loll
old doll old lad old load

Type these two lines a second time.

Are you returning the carriage with one clean movement? Are you putting the fingers of your left hand back on their home keys *without* looking at the keyboard? If you're not, practise again. You'll never be able to type fast unless you can do this.

Now type:

all dall doll load la
old all lala lolo lao

Look at what you have typed. Check it carefully against the book.

Mark the errors in the margin. If you have more than one error, type the exercise a second time.

Look at the chart:

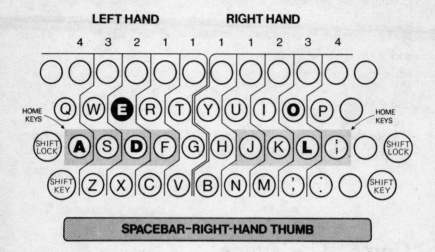

Your new letter is **e**. It is the most common letter in the English language. Once you have learnt to type it you will be able to type many more words.

You use the second finger of your left hand for this letter. Place all your fingers on their home keys. Type **d** with the second finger of your left hand. Then raise the second finger of your left hand and type **e**. Do this several times. Type:

d**e** d**e** d**e** d**e**

Now type:

al**e** old add do**e** l**e**d l**e**a l**e**e od**e**
ado **ee**l odd dad lad all d**ee** loo

(Are you returning the carriage smartly?)

d**e**al l**e**ad dol**e** dal**e** d**e**ad l**e**al lod**e**

(Type this line a second time.)

loll loll**ed** add add**ed** doodl**e** doodl**ed**
dol**e** dol**ed** load load**ed** ladl**e** ladl**ed**
addl**e** addl**ed** l**e**ad l**e**ad**ed** dol**e** dol**ed**

Look at what you have typed. Where you have had to type double letters, do they look the same? If the second one looks fainter than the first, practise again:

add l**ee** odd all d**ee** **e**lla loll d**e**ll doll

Make sure that you are typing double letters with two definite strokes.

Don't forget – date your sheet. Keep it in your file.

Unit 7   The letter **j**

Put your paper in the typewriter. Put your fingers on their home keys, and practise typing the letter **e** several times, returning the second finger of your left hand to its home key **d** each time.

Now practise typing the home keys, starting with the little finger of your left hand and finishing with the little finger of your right hand.

Type the following:

all old **e**ll dol**e** doll d**e**ll l**e**a
l**e**ad d**e**ad ladl**e** ladl**ed** odd **ee**l

Now type:

dol**ed** loll**ed** doll loll ad**e**l**e**
ad**e**la all al**e** dal**e** d**e**al l**e**ad

Check with the book. How many errors in the last line? More than one? Mark them in the margin. Type the line again if you have made more than one mistake.

Your new letter is **j**. Look at the chart:

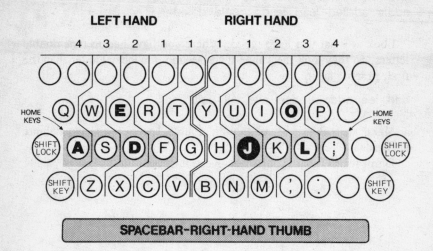

j is the home key for the first finger of your right hand. Put all the fingers of both hands on their home keys. Now strike **j** with the first finger of your right hand. Strike it several times with definite separate movements, saying the letter to yourself as you do so. Now type:

jo joll jojo jade jell jee jeel
jo joe jade jell joel jaded
jeel jeeled jell jelled jole

Look at the spaces between words. Are all the spaces equal? Are you tapping the spacebar with your right thumb without hesitation? Type this exercise. The mark ***** between the letters is to remind you to tap the spacebar:

j*o*j*l*j*a*j*e*j*d

Now type the same line, tapping the spacebar twice between letters:

j**o**j**l**j**a**j**e**j**d

Date your exercise sheet. Put it in your file.

Unit 8 The letter **s**

Practise typing the letter **j**. Type it several times, keeping your fingers on their home keys.
Type:

joll **j**ell **j**o **j**ade **j**ell

Repeat this once. Now type:

jojo jade joll jell jojo jade joll jell

Check what you've typed. Mark the number of errors in the margin. If there are more than one, repeat the last line.

In this unit, you're going to learn to type the letter **s**. Look at the chart:

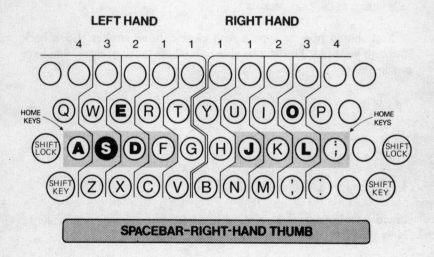

s is the home key for the third finger of the left hand. Put all your fingers on their home keys. With the third finger of your left hand, strike the key for **s**. Strike it several times with clear separate strikings, saying **s** to yourself as you do so. Now type:

sa sd se sj sl so se

ad lea see lee ell odd sad ale

ll less lose **sole** sell sale ease

odds does odes solo also sold doss

dose lads ella adds sole soda dell

addition of **s** to the letters you can type makes it possible for you

e simple sentences. Type the following:

sad ada sold old dolls
joe does so
joel loses lassoes
jo doodles
elsa sells loose salad
les saddles asses
della leads jo
jaded adele does less
ella also sells odd easels

You should now be typing with clear definite strokes. Look back through your file. You will be able to see how much progress you have made.

Unit 9   The letter **k**

Practise typing **s** several times, with all your fingers on their home keys. Now type the following as quickly as you can:

ja jo **s**o **s**a la lo je do le ja jo **s**o **s**a jd la lo

Repeat this once. Now type:

asses seas seed less seals leases lasso loses
loss lasso jess eases sees sells soles lasses
jesse sees lassoed seals salads less as sells

Your new letter is **k**. Look at the chart:

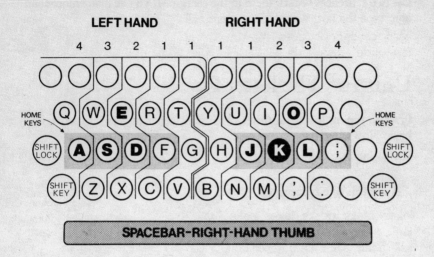

k is the home key for the second finger of your right hand. Strike it several times, saying it to yourself as you strike. Keep your other fingers on their home keys. Now type:

ka **k**o **k**j **k**s **k**l **k**e **k**d **k**a **k**o **k**j **k**l **k**e **k**d

Repeat this line once. Now type:

loo**k**s jo**k**es des**k** la**k**es **k**ale
keel **k**ola sa**k**e ja**k**e oa**k** as**k**
see**k** lea**k** slee**k** so**k**es lee**k**s

With **k** added to the list of letters you can type, more sentences are possible. Type these:

old ja**k**e as**k**ed ella
della jo**k**ed
ada sells lee**k**s
ella loo**k**s sad
jo sold oa**k** des**k**s
elsa sees a la**k**e
ada soa**k**s **k**ale

Check against the book. How many mistakes have you made in the last two sentences? Mark them in the margin. If you've made more than one, type the last two sentences again.

Unit 10   The letter **f**

Practise typing **k** several times, with your other fingers on their home keys. Now type:

ka **k**o **k**l **k**e **k**d **k**s **k**j

Type this line twice more. Now type:

jokes leeks desks lakes oaks
leak soak kale kola look eke
ask seek soke keel jake kell

Look at the keyboard chart. Your new letter is the letter **f**:

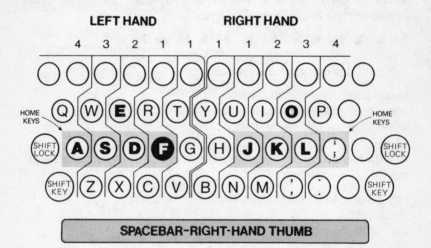

f is the home key for the first finger of your left hand. Practise typing it several times, saying it to yourself as you type it. Keep the other fingers of both hands on their home keys.

Now type these words:

fakes jaffas jeff fees fled
floods sofas flasks flak off
flees fleas floss false safe
safes foal food loaf fold of
falls fads fed fades feel foe
faddle flook folk fools flo

And now these sentences:

jeff saddled a foal
les sold a flask of ale
flo fell off a sofa
all deaf folk fled
jeff sold jaffas

Are you keeping your eyes on the book while you are typing? Concentrate on this.

Check these sentences against the book. Note in the margin the number of errors you have made. If you have made more than one error, type the sentences again, paying particular attention to looking at the book – not at your fingers or your typewriter.

Unit 11 The semicolon (;)

Type the letter **f** several times, with your other fingers on their home keys. Now type:

ff fa fs fd fe fj fk fl fo

Type this line once again. Now type these words:

off of foe fee fed oaf foe flo
jeff feel fled fade fools folk
flake fold fall flea safe loaf

Check these words against the book. Mark the errors you've made. If you have made no errors, you are making such good progress that you'll soon be able to type anything without hesitation. If you have only one error, you are still doing well. If you have more than one, type the exercise again. To type well, you must learn to type each key without hesitation. Don't go on until you have mastered this exercise.

Now look at the keyboard chart. The new key for you to learn is ;. The semicolon isn't used as much as the letter keys; but you need to learn it at this stage as it is one of the home keys. Look at the chart:

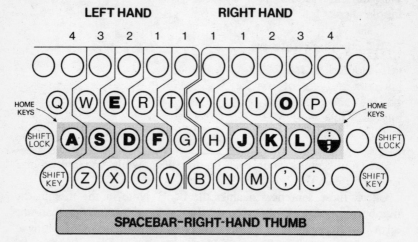

The semicolon is the home key for the little finger of your right hand. Type it several times, with your other fingers on their home keys.

You have now learnt all the home keys for both hands.

Type the following;

asdf ;lkj a; s; d; f; l; k; j;
e; o; de lo ;de ;lo ;a ;f ;j ;

This is a fairly difficult exercise. Don't worry if you are typing slightly more slowly than you did when you typed words. Now type:

jake sells flasks; so does flo
a load falls off;
saddle a foal;
feel safe;
sell a sofa;
saddle asses;
jeff fled;
asses flee; so do fools

Check this against the book. Type again any words that contain an error.

Are you keeping all your exercises in your folder? Look back at what you have typed. You can see how much progress you have made.

Unit 12   The letter **t**

Type the key for **;** several times, with your other fingers on their home keys. Now type:

asdf ;lkj asdf ;lkj;
a; s; d; f; j; k; l;

Repeat these two lines once. Now type:

food; jaffas; a loaf; leeks; kale;
a flask; ale; foals; asses; fools;
sell; seek; flee; fall; soak; ask;

Check what you have typed against the book. Mark any mistakes. Retype any line in which there is an error.

Your new letter is **t**. Look at the keyboard chart:

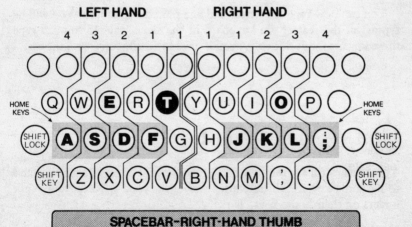

To type the letter **t** a different kind of reach is needed. Use the first finger of your left hand and reach up and to the right to strike **t**. When you have struck the new letter, return your finger to its home key **f**. With your other fingers on their home keys, strike **t** several times while you are looking at the keyboard. Now do the same thing with your eyes closed, saying the letter to yourself as you do so. Look back at the book, and type:

ft dt st at ;t lt kt jt ot et

Type this line again. Now type these words:

total take took kate otto too to
tea tot talk task loot toot dote
fat aft toe toad foot teat tells
told tall lest last lost lot toe

Now type these sentences:

otto told kate a joke;
kate took a lot of tea;
tessa took a set of skates off a stall;
jake saddled a fat foal;
ted asked a tall lad;
les tootled off;
tod tested a set of loose seeds;

You can now type ten letters and one punctuation mark. You will be typing all the rest of the keyboard in the same way. If you can type these keys without difficulty, you'll have little difficulty with the rest.

Unit 13 The letter **h**

Type the key for **t** several times. Return the first finger of your left hand to its home key **f** each time after you have typed **t**. Keep your other fingers on their home keys. Type:

at st dt ft jt kt lt ;t ot et

Are you returning your fingers to their home keys?

Repeat this line, typing more slowly than usual and concentrating on returning your fingers to their home keys. Now type:

otto total tot toot to too teat
ta tat tattle tootle total test
tote stet take jet lot toast at

Check what you have typed against the book. Mark any errors you have made. If you have made more than one, type each word containing a mistake three times.

Look at the chart:

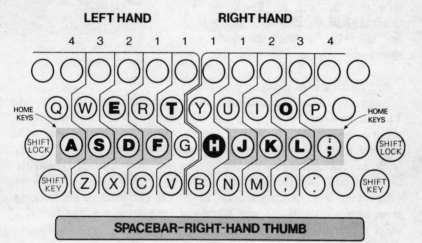

Your new letter is the letter **h**. It is typed with the first finger of your right hand, but the reach is different from those you have learnt before. To type **h**, you move the first finger sideways from its home key **j**. Directly you have typed **h**, move the first finger of your right hand back to its home key **j**. With all your other fingers on their home keys type **jhj jhj jhj** several times.

Now type:

ha **h**s **h**d **h**e **h**f **h**t **h**j **h**k **h**l **h**o **h**;

Repeat this line. Now type these words:

half t**h**at **h**at**h** deat**h** oat**h** dot**h** doet**h** lot**h** e**h**

loathe sheath sheet shoot hash heath he shoe
tooth hoot head those teeth shoo she hoe hot
ho ha tho hothead hot hat has had the theses

Now that you can type **h**, you can type many more sentences. Type
these:

he has sold half a loaf as food
he shooed the asses off the heath
hotheaded hal shot the foal
kate took those; tessa sold these
seth held a left shoe
take that hat off the head
the ale has soaked the old leaf
ask the lass to heat the flask
she feels safe as the fool has fled

Put your sheet of paper in your file.

Before you start the next unit, make a backing sheet for yourself.
This can be a sheet of paper or thin card slightly wider than the sheet of
paper on which you are typing. You make a mark on it about one inch
from the foot. When you next put a sheet of paper into your typewriter,
lay it on your backing sheet, and put the two sheets into the typewriter
together, with the backing sheet next to the roller. This helps to stop
your typing from making dents in the roller. The mark on the backing
sheet also helps you to notice when you are getting near the foot of a
sheet of paper. When this happens, take the paper out of the typewriter, and put in a fresh sheet.

Unit 14   Capital letters

Practise typing **h**, moving the first finger of your right hand from its
home key **j** sideways to the letter **h**. Return your finger to **j** after each
typing. Keep your other fingers on their home keys. Type the
following:

he ha ho ah eh oh hot hat the hoe has hod had

Repeat this line once, typing as fast as you possibly can. Now type:

that head josh shot hest seth half hake hold
shod tosh shed dash lash oath hath hats hate

Type these lines again, concentrating on even rhythmic typewriting. The words are all the same length, and you should not find this difficult.

Look at the chart:

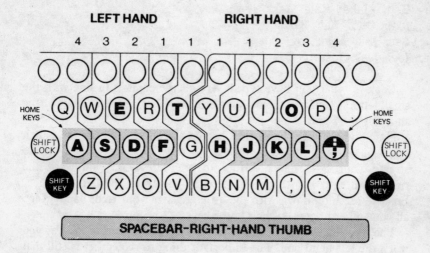

The key you're going to learn to type this time is not a new letter or punctuation mark. It is the **shift key**. Its function is to make it possible for you to type capital letters. There are two shift keys. The one you are going to learn first is the one to the left of and below the letter **a**. You use the fourth finger of your left hand for this.

Put your fingers on their home keys. Reach down and to the left with the little finger of your left hand, and push the shift key down. This is a different movement from the one you use for the ordinary keys. It takes more effort. To make it work properly, do it step by step:

1. Type the letter **j**.
2. Reach with your little finger down to the left shift key. Press it and hold it down.
3. Type the letter **j**.
4. Release the shift key with the little finger of your left hand.

The most important thing to remember is to **hold the shift key down while you type the capital letter**. Now type:

jJ hH jJ kK lL oO ;:

You'll notice that when the shift key is held down the key for ; types :.

The ways in which the **colon** and semicolon are used as punctuation marks will be dealt with in Unit 33. At present all you need to do is to learn to type them when you see them in the book. Type:

Hetta: Jake: Kate: Leo:
Joel: Otto: Hal: Kes:
Les: Jeff: Lola: Jo:
Joe: Jess: Jesse:

Look at what you have typed. Are all the capitals in line with the small letters? If any of them aren't, it means that you have let go of the shift key too soon.

Now find the **right-hand shift key** on the chart. You use the fourth finger of your right hand to work it. On most typewriters, you have to stretch your little finger farther to one side when you work the right-hand shift key than you do when you work the left-hand one. Practise reaching down with the little finger of your right hand. Keep all your other fingers on their home keys.

The way you work the right-hand shift key is the same as the way you work the left-hand one. The important thing to remember is still that you must *hold* the shift key down while you type the letter you want to be in capitals. Using the right-hand shift key where necessary, type the following:

aA sS dD fF eE tT fF

Repeat this line once. Now type these words:

Tessa Adele Sal Flo Ed
Asa Theo Elsa Stella
Sholto Ada Ethel Dot
Adela Ella Seth Della

Look at what you have typed to make sure that the capital letters are in line with the other letters. If they're not, type this exercise again, paying particular attention to holding down the shift key while you are typing the capital letters.

You have now learnt to use both the left-hand and right-hand shift keys. The next exercise will give you more practice in using them. In this exercise, though, you have to decide *which* shift key to use! You use the left-hand one for any key that is typed with your right hand, and the right-hand one for any key that is typed with the left hand. Type these words:

Ed **J**ake **T**ed **J**o **A**da **E**lla **K**es **S**al **L**es

Type this line once more. Now type these sentences:

Tell **E**thel to sell the ladles to **E**d
Hold the saddle: the foal has fled
Jake sat at the stall: **L**es tootled off
Ted took the shade off
Ask **J**oel to look at the tooth
He took a flask of tea to **E**lsa
She told a lot of jokes to old **O**tto
Folk hate **J**oe: he has a lot of foes
Ella fell off the shed
Ada eats jaffas; so does **J**o
Tessa added the totals of the test

Remember – you need a capital letter at the beginning of each sentence.

Are you using your backing sheet?

Unit 15   The full stop (.)

Type the following:

Ja **S**; **D**; **E**k t: **O**h **L**d **E**e **T**o **D**k **K**d

Repeat this line once. Look at the exercise, and check it carefully against the book. You should now be able to type capital letters without difficulty. If you have made more than one mistake, type the exercise again, paying particular attention to holding down the shift key.

Look at the keyboard chart:

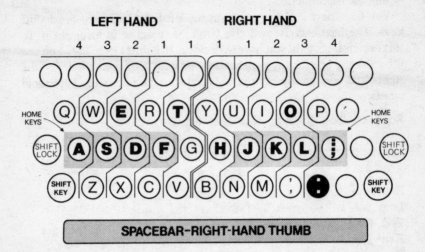

The new key for you to learn is that for the **full stop**. To type it you use the fourth finger of your right hand. You have to move this finger downwards and slightly to the left to strike the **full stop**. Try this movement once or twice, returning the finger to its home key ; after each strike, and keeping all the other fingers on their home keys. Now type:

a. s. d. e. f. t. h. j. k. l. o. ;.

Repeat this line once.

The full stop is typed at the end of most sentences. At the end of a sentence you leave two spaces by tapping the spacebar twice. The mark * is to remind you to tap the spacebar. Type the following:

Ted fell off.**Jake told Tess.
Jo sold the hat.**Ada ate a lot.
Ed set the test.**Al looks sad.

Take the paper out of your typewriter and look at the back of it. A common fault in typing the full stop is to type it too hard so that it dents the paper. If you are doing this, try to strike it more lightly as you type these sentences:

Jake feels safe.**Ted lost a shoe.
Take the teaset.**Ed has a lot.
Jo sees the oaks.**So does Tess.
Otto hates the sea.**Joel has left.
He looks odd.**So does she.

Look at what you have typed. Are you leaving the right number of spaces at the end of each sentence?

Are you using your backing sheet?

Unit 16   The letter **i**

Type the following. Remember to leave two spaces at the end of a sentence:

She sells seashells.**He sells seashells.

Repeat this line twice, typing as fast as you possibly can. Now type:

Ted ate. Jake fled. Ada added.
Joe looked. Elsa fell. Otto asked.
Ella sold. Della dealt. Sal shot.

Look at the chart:

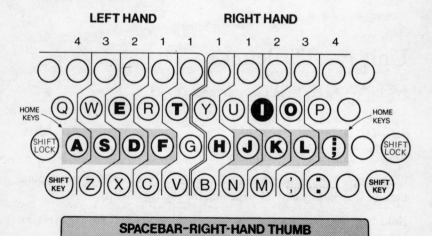

Your new key is the letter **i**. It is typed with the second finger of the right hand. Put all your fingers on their home keys. Reach with the second finger of your right hand up from **k** and slightly to the left. Strike **i**, and return your finger to its home key **k** immediately. Practise doing this several times, keeping your other fingers on their home keys. Now type:

is id it if Di hi aid die ide did tie
ill Ida fie Sid lid hit hid; hide
his its sit lit fit ilk sill diseases
silk site side said tiff hill killed;
till file Sallie jiff Isaiah thistles

Now type these sentences:

Eddie tilled the side of the hill.
Jill filled the flask.
The field has a lot of thistles.
Joel jilted Sallie.
Ailsa disliked the idea.
She died of the disease.
That idiot hit the sill.

You should be able to type them without hesitation.

Unit 17   The letter **r**

Practise typing the letter **i** several times. Type:

idiot idea iota dial faith hit lido
lied Lil Leila side diss hid jilted
idealise shift died kill saith said

Now type these sentences. They are all short. Concentrate on typing the full stop lightly and on returning the carriage swiftly:

Hold it.
Set it off.

Hide it.
Till the field.
He is idle.
It is ideal.
Take it aside.
He is ill.

Check what you have typed, and mark any errors. How quickly did
you return the carriage?

Now look at the chart:

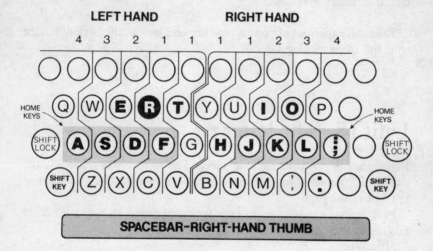

Your new letter is **r**. To type it, move the first finger of your left hand
up from its home key **f** and slightly to the left. Practise typing this
several times with all your other fingers on their home keys. Say the
letter to yourself as you do so. Type:

error err are far for red terror
or rare farther rose sore rot re
rat fort free jar dark jerk fair
air lard hard fret trifle reader
dare rake rill joker Rose Teresa
fear either jester jotter afraid
roof striker Dora tree other tor

Your exercises are getting longer. They shouldn't be taking you much longer to type, though. You should be developing speed and be responding quickly to the sight of the letter in the book.

Now type these sentences:

Teresa is terrified of the dark.
Terror strikes her.
Rosie feels safer there.
Dora stored the other jar.
Her foot is sore after the hard task.
Either the lads or their father are there.
Iris has short red hair.

Take the paper out of your typewriter and look at the back of it. Are your full stops making a dent?

Unit 18   The letter **n**

Remember to use your backing sheet. The farther you work through this book, the more you will need to have a warning that you are near the foot of the page.

Practise typing the letter **r**. Type it several times, with all your other fingers on their home keys.

Now type:

hard rare errs fare fore read rise
real lair roar lair fear road rose
are; ore; rat; oar; for; far; rot;

And now these sentences:

This larder is dark.
Rose is a jester.
Take shelter: it is late.
Rolf realised it too late.
Rosalie is a liar.
There are three trees there.
The red rose is rare.

Look at the chart:

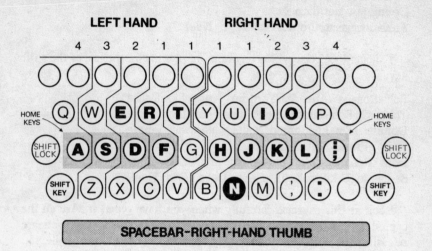

Your new letter is **n**. It is typed with the first finger of the right hand. To type it, reach down and slightly to the left from **j**. Type **n**, and return your finger to its home key **j**. Practise doing this several times with all your other fingers on their home keys.

Now type:

a**n** s**n** d**n** e**n** f**n** r**n** t**n** h**n** j**n** k**n** i**n** l**n** o**n** ;**n** .**n**
na **n**s **n**d **n**e **n**f **n**r **n**t **n**h **n**j **n**k **n**i **n**l **n**o **n**; **n**.

Now type these words:

A**nn** i**nn**er si**n** and John loa**n** da**n**k ofte**n**
si**nn**er i**n**k Ke**n**t sa**n**d fa**n** he**nn**a fi**n**e o**n**
De**nn**is liste**n** hidde**n** do**n**or di**nn**er sa**n**e
Je**nn**ie se**nn**a fi**n**d fi**n** **n**atio**n** ta**n**k Joa**n**
ri**n**k de**n** de**n**se Fra**n**k fa**nn**ed si**n**k li**n**er

And now these sentences:

Do**n**ald has se**n**t a fra**n**k letter to De**nn**is.
Ia**n** le**n**t I**n**es his I**n**dia**n** i**n**k.
The li**n**er sa**n**k **n**ear **n**orth Ke**n**t.

Ron did a ton on the Norfolk road.
There is a dent in the stainless steel sink.
Dennis is not honest.
Anne does not often listen to Noel.

This next exercise will give you more practice in the use of the shift key:

Rolf Rosalie Ann Jane Anne Janet Flo Tessa
Theresa Rose Rosa Neil Janie Ian John Jane
Dennis Donald Ronald Kate Katherine Jennie
Rosie Frank Jeff Edna Ella Stella Iris Ron
Dora Rosa Roddie Linda Sal Jake Otto Ethel
Sadie Joel Kath Keith Delia Della Ada Noel

Look at this exercise carefully when you have typed it. Are all the capital letters in alignment? If they're not, it means that you are releasing the shift key too quickly. It must be *held down* while you strike the letter.

Unit 19   The letter **w**

Practise the last letter you learnt – **n**. Type it several times, saying it to yourself as you do so. Now type:

lank sodden into net hand near fanned sink;
roan liner nil Edna ton done Linda lent inn
near Norfolk land rink Ian donor dinner Don
Rhona nil sank din listen lenten dank send;

And now these sentences:

A loan does not aid Jennie.
Janet had sole for dinner.
The lino is sodden; so is the floor.
The roan horse is on loan to Ron.
Lend a hand to John.
Do not sit near the rink: it is not safe.

Look at the chart:

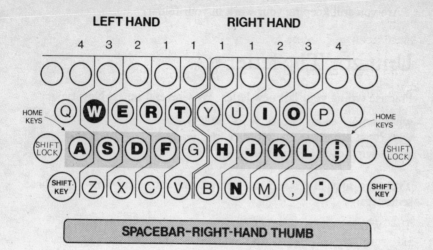

Your new letter is **w**. This is typed with the third finger of your left hand – the wedding-ring finger! To type it, you reach up and slightly to the left. Practise typing it several times, keeping your other fingers on their home keys.

Now type these words:

windo**w** **w**ant **w**ind **w**est flo**w**er flo**w** **w**ith
wend farro**w** sorro**w** **w**and **w**ither **w**ill **w**e
wanted **w**rites sho**w** **w**illo**w** **w**hither **w**ise
wish **w**it **w**ho **w**idth **w**aiter o**w**ner **w**ilder
whether **w**ido**w** **w**hite flo**w**er **w**hile **w**here

Now type these sentences:

The **w**hite flo**w**er **w**as **w**ithered.
Will **w**ent to **W**andsworth.
Thornton **W**ilder **w**as a **w**riter.
So **w**as Sha**w**.
Winifred **W**ilson is a **w**ido**w**.
Walter **W**alker **w**alked to the horse sho**w**.
He did not kno**w** **w**here his **w**ife **w**as.
He **w**anted to see a **W**estern; so did **W**ilfred.
He is **w**ise: he kno**w**s ho**w** to **w**ait.

I **w**ent to **W**est **W**ales for a **w**eek.

Are you still keeping your work in your folder?

Unit 20   The letter **u**

Practise typing your last new letter – **w** – several times. Now type:

what **w**hen **w**ear **w**ord **w**ore **w**ill **w**ast
with **w**ist **w**ind **w**ore **w**ere **w**ide **w**ait
woe; **w**in; owe; own; **w**on; **w**it;

Type the first line again, as fast as you can. And now type these sentences:

The wind shakes the willows.
He was one of those who walked to Jarrow.
She knew who her friends were.
He knows what he wants.
He will let her know when.
The white kitten sat on the windowsill.
He does not know what he owns.
Wilde was known for his wit.

Look at the chart:

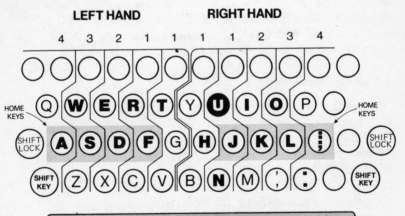

Your new letter is **u**. To type it, you use the first finger of your right hand. You reach up and slightly to the left from your home key **j**; strike **u**; and return your finger to **j**. Do this several times, keeping your other fingers on their home keys.

Type these words:

unto fun fur unsure unusual out untrue
unuttered unused nurture rust rusk nut
truths Ursula untuneful four flute our
just unhurt Truro rouse unsound unjust
luke house sunder runner ruin treasure

Check the last two lines carefully against the book. Mark any errors in the margin. If you have made a mistake, type both lines again, concentrating on typing more slowly and more rhythmically.

Now type these sentences:

It is unusual for Louise to run out of flour.
The house in south Dundee is in ruins.
Laurie is a surefooted runner.
Julian is untruthful.
That lute has an untuneful sound.
Ursula was nurtured on rusks.
That nut has rusted: it is unsafe.
Julia found treasure in the old hut.
He went on a tour to Ullswater in June.
The stout is unusual.
The tun has stood out in the sun.

Are you remembering to use a backing sheet? Don't forget to add the date to any second sheet of paper you use.

Unit 21   The letter **c**

Type this list of all the characters you have learnt so far:

asdf;lkjwertoiuhn.**ASDF:LKJWERTOIUHN.

Repeat this line once. Check to make sure that the capital letters are all right – did you type them so that they were all on the same level? If not, you are not holding the shift key down long enough.

Now type these words:

lute dust rut nutrition tour
ours use usual ritual Julian
rue Ruth sure null ruse shun

And now these sentences:

Ruth was found out.
It is an unusual ritual.
Truro has a lot of sunshine.
Luton is dull.
Store the four utensils on the wooden shelf.
He hit his shoulder: it hurt.
The sound in the tunnel was hushed.

Look at the chart:

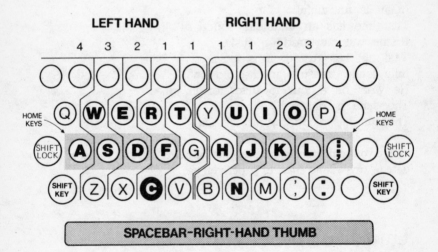

Your new letter is **c**. You type it with the first finger of your left hand. Type the home key **f**; reach down and slightly to the left, and type **c**;

and return your first finger immediately to its home key. Practise doing
this several times with all all your other fingers on their home keys.

Now type:

accident classic cocoa click cuckoo
incidence chocolate chicken cadence
catch couch cricket science act cut
which each such clench choice catch

And now these sentences:

The cricket coach hit his wicket.
Celia chose cocoa and a scone.
We can choose which chocolate we like.
For lunch he cooked chicken and cauliflower.
Cathie chose a coloured cotton.
Clara called in for a chat.
The clock struck once.
Charlie decided on iced coffee.
The choice is claret or cider or Scotch.
The child cut his knuckle on the can.
The cock crowed.
The hen cackled and clucked.
She had just hatched a clutch of chickens.

Check:

Are you using a backing sheet?
Are you dating what you type?
Are you keeping it in your file?

You're marvellous!

Unit 22   The letter m

Type this list of words one under the other, concentrating on returning
the carriage quickly and returning your fingers to their home keys
without looking at the keyboard:

cat	wen**ch**
cute	**c**lo**ck**
cad	**ch**o**c**kful
colour	in**ch**
lu**ck**	**c**lut**ch**
cow	**c**riti**c**
on**ce**	**c**hart
s**c**one	**c**hart

Now type these sentences:

Carol and Cecile danced the cancan.
Colin could not decide which cake to choose.
The colt cantered to the croft fence.
He is critical of the classics.
Catch as catch can is a kind of contest.
The cat clawed at the curtain.
The local council decided to consult the court.

Look at the chart:

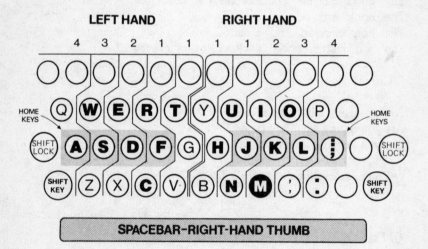

Your new letter is **m**. You type it with the second finger of your right hand. Strike the home key **k**. Then reach down and slightly to the left and strike **m** several times, keeping your other fingers on their home keys. Now type:

mu**m** **mim**osa **m**ur**m**ur **m**an **mem**orise el**ms** **M**rs;
memories **m**ausoleu**m** **m**ini**m**u**m** **m**o**m**ent **m**a**mm**al
mo**m**entu**m** **m**ini**m** **m**useu**m** **m**a**mm**oth **m**isti**m**e **m**e
milli**m**etre **m**a**mm**a **m**u**mm**ers **m**ediu**m** co**mm**its;

Some of the following sentences take two lines. Return the carriage when you get to the end of the line, and go on typing:

The **m**onu**m**ent in the **m**useu**m** **m**ade her think of
her ti**m**e in **M**alta.
Mrs Ada**ms** **m**et **M**aria **M**cIntosh on Ha**m** Co**mm**on.
She **m**easured the **m**ini**m**u**m** a**m**ount of **m**ilk.
The **m**e**m**orial co**mm**e**m**orated co**mm**issioned
officers of the **m**ilitia.
Ma**m**ie **m**ade a **m**istake and **m**isti**m**ed the race.
Few **m**en and wo**m**en are co**mm**itted to the **m**ission.
In ter**m**ti**m**e he studies co**mm**erce and **m**athe**m**atics.
In a **m**o**m**ent **M**rs **M**ac**M**illan **m**ade a **m**ushroo**m**
o**m**elette.

Look at what you have typed to see whether the letters are of the same darkness. If some are lighter than others, you're typing too quickly. Type one sentence again, concentrating this time on an even rhythmic touch.

Unit 23   The letter **g**

Your last new letter was **m**. Practise typing this several times. Now type:

co**mm**ission **m**ediu**m** co**mm**erce co**mm**e**m**orate co**mm**a
co**mm**on **m**ission **M**a**mm**on **m**u**mm**ified Adam **m**istake
misname **m**isnomer **M**iss **M**rs centi**m**etre **m**iracle

Check what you have typed against the book. Mark any errors in the margin. Retype any line in which there is a mistake.

Now type:

She eats marmalade or Marmite with her toast.
Marian made a mess with the mud.
Mimosa makes more smell than elm trees.
The middle marker measured ten millimetres.
Mark made a name for himself as a mathematician.
The mammoth ornament meant much to Miss Maddock.

Now look at the chart:

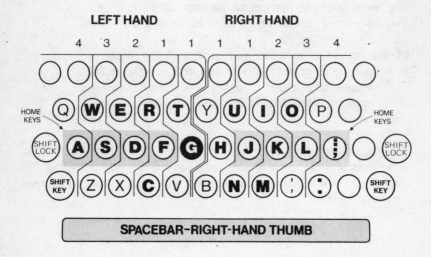

Your new letter is **g**. You type this with the first finger of your left hand. Strike the home key **f**. Reach with the finger to the right. Strike **g**. Return the finger to the home key. Practise typing **g** several times with all your other fingers on their home keys.

Now type:

giggle dog dagger getting eight Meg;
gorge gagging going German enough go
God gone goggle green hugging though
rough rogue log digger leg anger rag

Now type these sentences.

Me**g** gi**gg**led when **G**eor**g**e made a **g**a**g**.
The do**g** was di**gg**in**g** in the **g**arden.
Gemma **g**ot ei**g**hteen e**gg**s from **G**re**gg**s the **G**rocers.
Gill chan**g**ed **g**ear as the li**g**hts were **g**reen.
Gre**g** was rou**g**h enou**g**h at ru**gg**er.
Greta thou**g**ht the **g**olfers were at the ei**g**hth
green.
Gerald had **g**one to **G**reece with **G**loria.
A **g**a**gg**le of **g**eese waddled to the **g**ara**g**e.

Before you put your papers away, look back through your file. You
can see how much progress you have made.

Because you are getting on so well, don't feel you can skip some of
the exercises. If you're getting on *really* well, the exercises won't take
you long to type anyway.

Unit 24   The letter **y**

Practise typing the letter **g** several times. Then type:

e**gg** **g**a**g** **g**ad do**g** ho**g** lo**g** so**g** na**g** di**g**
fo**g** no**g** jo**g** le**g** sa**g** ra**g** ta**g** e**g**o ti**g**
fi**g** na**g** mu**g** hu**g** lu**g** tu**g** ru**g** wa**g** wi**g**

Check the last line for any errors. Mark them in the margin. Retype a
whole line of any word in which you have made a mistake.

Now type these sentences:

It was light enough for him to see through his
goggles.
Nigel has gone to Glasgow for eight weeks.
After the fight the gingerhaired man was
groaning in the gutter.
The dog ran like greased lightning.
It goes against the grain.

Look at the chart:

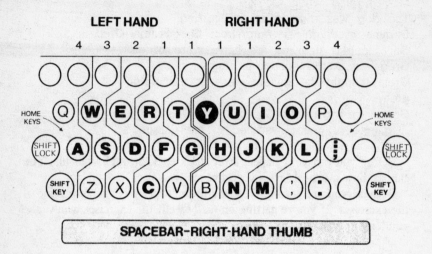

Your new letter is **y**. It is typed with the first finger of your right hand. Type the home key **j**. Reach up and to the left and strike **y**. Return your finger immediately to the home key. Practise this several times with your other fingers on their home keys.

Now type:

alle**y**wa**y** **y**oghurt **y**okel **y**oung C**y**nthia **y**ou
yo**y**o worr**y** **y**esterda**y** Monda**y** Jimm**y** **y**ellow
hurr**y** **y**ounger **y**et **y**ams **y**ard **y**oke **Y**ork **y**e

Now type these sentences:

Sall**y** lost her **y**ellow **y**o**y**o **y**esterda**y**.
Jimm**y** has man**y** to**y** **y**achts.
Monda**y**s and Tuesda**y**s are good da**y**s for **y**ou to
carr**y** out **y**our aims.
Mr **Y**ates **y**elled at his **y**oung son.
The cat la**y** in the alle**y**wa**y** all da**y**.
Each da**y** Lad**y** Fole**y** takes her tin**y** dog to the
yard.
C**y**nthia is hurr**y**ing: Ka**y** has not **y**et started.

You can now type all these characters:

asdf;lkjwertoiuhnmgyc.

Type them three times as quickly as you can.

Unit 25   The shift lock

Look at the chart:

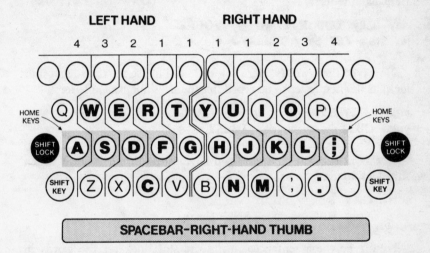

Above the shift keys you'll see two keys that are not marked with any character – though they may be labelled **shift lock**. There is, on most typewriters, one at the left-hand side of the machine and one at the right. They are operated with the little finger. Their function is to hold down the shift key so that you can type several capital letters straight off without having to keep pushing down the shift key.

The two shift locks work in exactly the same way: whether you press down the left-hand or the right-hand one, the effect is the same. Which key you use depends on which hand you need to use for the next key you have to strike. If you want to type the word **YOU** all in capital letters, you use the left-hand shift lock so that your right hand is ready to strike the **Y** of **YOU**. If you want to type **CAT** in capital letters, you use the right-hand shift lock so that your left hand is ready to strike the **C** of **CAT**.

To operate the shift lock, use the little finger and press the key right down. Unlike other keys, it will stay down. And as long as the shift lock is down, all the characters you type will be capitals. When you want to switch back to ordinary, small letters, you have to press down a **shift key**. Pressing down either shift key releases the shift lock.

Practise pressing down the shift lock several times, and then practise depressing the shift key to release it. Now type these words using the shift lock to type the capitals. In this first group you will use the left-hand shift lock, as the first letter to be typed in capitals is a right-hand letter:

day daily **YOU K**ay aye jay **YOURS**
jay way **YES S**ally **YELLOW** yields

Now type these words. Here you will need to use the right-hand shift lock, as the first letter to be typed in capitals is a left-hand letter:

yellowy **SWAY** yarn yields **SWARMS**
yoga **CUTTY** lay heyday **DAISY** eye

In this next batch of words, you have to decide for yourself which shift lock to use:

sorry **GAY S**idney **SILLY** yet lily
key kingly **HAY** yacht **YANK H**arry

Now type these sentences, using the shift lock for the words in capital letters:

Knit the **YOKE** with this gay yarn.
Jersey cows yield a **YELLOWY** milk.
It is twenty years since I saw **RODDY RILEY**.
It is easy to say **YES**.
Gary has lost the KEY of the yard.

When you use the shift lock remember:

The colon is a shift-key character.
The key for the full stop is the same whether the shift key is depressed or not.

Unit 26 The letter **v**

Practise working the shift lock several times. Then type the following:

Mr **J C Y**oung came yesterday.
The **MC** and **MM** are awarded for gallantry.
All I want to know is **WHY**.
This means **YOU**.
NSCR stands for National Society for Cancer
Relief.

Now look at your keyboard chart:

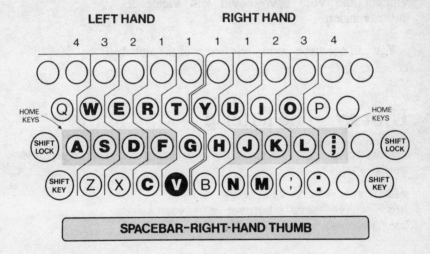

Your new letter is **v**. This is typed with the first finger of your left hand. To type it, strike the home key **f**. Then reach down and to the right and strike **v**. Return your finger to **f** immediately. Practise striking **v** several times with your other fingers on their home keys.

Now type these words:

vi**v**acious **v**eracity e**v**ery E**v**e E**v**elyn e**v**ent
vi**v**isection in**v**ol**v**e **v**al**v**e a**v**enue ha**v**e **v**at
wi**v**es **v**ent **v**iew **v**i**v**id **v**er**v**e **v**alue **v**illage
mo**v**ement **v**oti**v**e e**v**en **v**ery **v**intner **V**incent

And now these sentences:

The River **V**er runs near **V**erulamium.
The **V**incents li**v**e in **V**ictoria A**v**enue.
Vivienne **v**isited E**v**elyn e**v**ery day.
Veronica had arranged to **v**iew the **V**ictorian
villa that e**v**ening.
From the **v**illage the **v**iew o**v**er the **v**alley was
magnificent.
The **v**alue of tra**v**el is e**v**ident after you ha**v**e
arri**v**ed.
Valerie is a **viv**acious ci**v**il ser**v**ant.
Safety **v**al**v**es sa**v**e **v**ery many li**v**es.
Vincent and **V**era ha**v**e ne**v**er told **V**ictor of
the re**v**olution.

You can now type twenty-one letters of the alphabet!

Unit 27   The letter **p**

Practise typing your last new letter **v** several times. Then type these
words:

venue **v**ery e**v**ery **v**alid **v**alue **v**ale
wo**v**e wea**v**e wa**v**e where**v**er **v**ow **v**ase
lo**v**e re**v**ol**v**er **v**erity **v**ain **v**an **v**et

Check the last line against this book. Mark any errors in the margin.
Type any word containing a mistake six times before you go on to type
these sentences:

The valet wore a velvet livery of vivid colours.
They have several scents: you can choose violet
or lavender.
For lunch he had veal cutlets Viennoise and a
vanilla ice.
His intervention saved Valerie from a violent and
savage attack.
Some call virtues what others call vices.

Look at the chart:

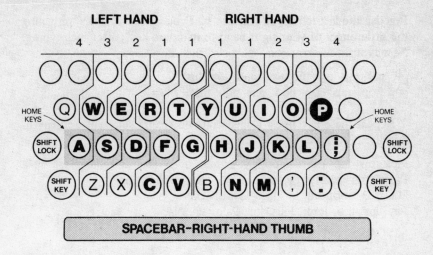

Your new letter is **p**. This is typed with the little finger of your right hand. To type it, reach up and slightly to the left. Type **p;p;** several times, keeping your other fingers on their home keys all the time.

Now type these words:

pu**pp**y **p**o**pp**et **p**o**pp**ing **p**o**p**e **p**o**pp**y;
pin **p**i**pp**in **p**utting **p**oo**p**; a**pp**les;
pe**pp**er **p**o**p**corn da**pp**er su**pp**er **p**ot
pet sa**pp**er **p**aper; **p**u**p**il; **p**o**pp**er;

Now type these sentences:

Peter **P**i**p**er **p**icked a **p**eck of **p**ickled **p**e**pp**er;
A **p**eck of **p**ickled **p**e**pp**er **P**eter **P**i**p**er **p**icked.
A **p**ilfering **p**ick**p**ocket **p**icked the **p**acket from
her **p**ocket.
The **p**ortly **p**rinter **p**ied the **p**ica ty**p**e.
The **p**orter **p**ut the **p**ack on the **p**it **p**ony.
Plenty of **p**eople **p**ay for **p**rinted **p**apers.

Check on the capital letters in these sentences – are they in line? Or are you releasing the shift key too quickly?

Unit 28   The letter **x**

Practise the last letter you learnt – **p**. Type it several times, returning the little finger of your right hand to its home key ; after each typing. Now type:

pit **p**ot ta**p** ti**p** **p**ut a**p**t **p**ad fo**p** li**p**
co**p** to**p** ra**p** sa**p** **p**od **p**in **p**un ma**p** mo**p**

   Repeat these two lines. Concentrate on typing smoothly and rhyth-mically. Now type these sentences:

Pick up the purple poppy petals from the path.
Paste the pretty picture on to the puce paper.
Put the peppers in the pewter pot.
Pay for the Pink Pills for Pale People.
Pin the packet to your pink pinafore.

   Now look at the chart:

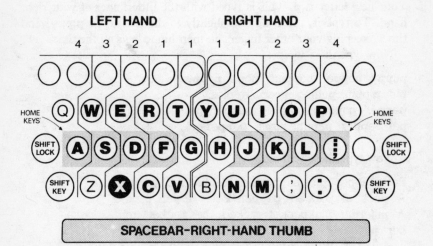

Your new letter is **x**. It is typed with the second finger of your left hand. Type **d**. Reach down slightly to the left to type **x**. Return your finger immediately to its home key **d**. Practise this several times, keeping your other fingers on their home keys. Now type these words:

extra excellent exemplary exit exigency
six sixty vexed annexe texture axe axis
saxe dexterity mixture lexicon next sex
pox toxic Rex Exeter vixen Oxford foxes

And now these sentences:

The extra exercises were excellent.
The vexed sexton was an expert xylophonist.
Six oxen are worth sixty foxes.
The Oxford cox expected to catch the Exeter
express.
Use the next exit to reach the annexe.
Six excisemen went on the next excursion.
The exact extent of the excess mixture is not
evident.

Compare the last sentence with this book. Mark any errors in the
margin. If you have made a mistake, type the sentence again.

Unit 29 The comma (,)

Practise typing your last letter – x. Type the letters **dex** several times.
Then type these words:

mix vex pax tax fix sex axe pox exe   .

Type this line once more. Concentrate on typing rhythmically. You
shouldn't have any difficulty with this exercise.
Now type these sentences:

The executive fixed the maximum tax.
The exhaust of the taxi gave out a noxious fume.
The expert took exception to the exact example.
Fix the extent of the six exercises for the next
examination.
The extent of the excavation exceeded their
expectations.

Look at the chart:

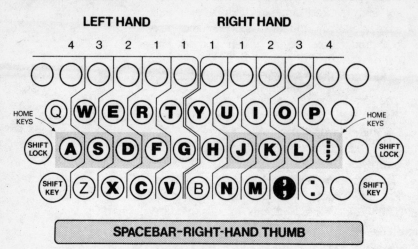

Your new character is the comma (,). On most machines, the shift-key character for the comma is also a comma. But look carefully at your own machine. On some typewriters, the shift-key character for the comma is the question mark.

To type the comma, strike the letter **l** with the third finger of the right hand. Reach down and slightly to the left and strike the key for the comma. Return your finger immediately to its home key **l**. Practise this movement several times with all your other fingers on their home keys.

After striking the comma you tap the spacebar once. Keeping this in mind, type the following sentences:

You may,*of course,*know this.
I want to know why,*what,*when,*and where.
Oh,*Shenandoah,*I long to hear you.
Adieu,*adieu,*kind friends,*adieu,*adieu,*adieu.
To strive,*to seek,*to find,*and not to yield.
He was a nasty,*vicious,*angry,*loathsome man.
They were all there: old ones,*young ones,*nice
ones,*nasty ones.

Check: the last two sentences should be compared with the book very carefully. Mark any errors in pencil. Type again any sentence in which you have made an error.

Unit 30　The letter q

Practise typing your last new key – the one for the comma. Make sure that your fingers stay on their home keys.

Now type the following:

and,*the,*are,*say,*too,*two,*can,
see,*you,*our,*her,*his,*let,*for,
its,*out,*why,*now,*way,*nor,*yet,
say,*one,*not,*him,*who,*was,*did,

Check this exercise very carefully. It contains nothing but simple common words. If you have made any errors, type the word in which you have made the mistake six times.

Now type these sentences:

Matthew, Mark, Luke, and John.
The drawer of her desk contained one file, two
sheets of dirty paper, six old pens, and a chewed
pencil.

You can now type these letters: a, c, d, e, f, g, h, i, j, k, l, m, n, o, p, r, s, t, u, v, w, x, y.

Type them all once, typing as fast as you can.

Look at the chart:

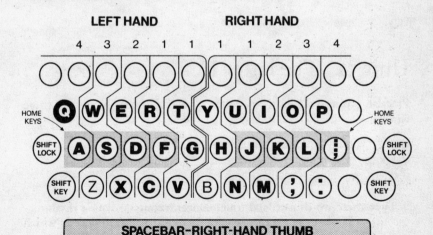

Your new letter is **q**. It is typed with the little finger of your left hand. Strike the key for **a**. Then reach up and slightly to the left and strike **q**. Return your finger to its home key **a** immediately. Practise striking **q** several times, keeping all your other fingers on their home keys.

Now type these words:

queer quick quite quiet quill
quips quell quids quack quaff
qualm quake quart quasi quays

And now these sentences:

The quins quickly quaffed the quince wine.
The querulous queen queried the sequence of
questions.
The quantity surveyor requested quality
equipment for the aqueduct.
Quentin Quinn queued for quills.
Queenie felt queasy after eating the quail.
He quietly queried the sequel to the question.
That is not a query or a question.

Before you go on to the next unit, take a look back at what you have typed. Are you returning the carriage quickly? Are your capital letters in alignment?

Unit 31   The letter **b**

Practise typing your last new letter **q** several times. Now type these words:

qualify quality queried equalled
quicken quietly quested inquests
request queuing squalid inquired

Type these words a second time, concentrating on typing rhythmically and evenly. Check the second typing for any errors. Mark them in pencil in the margin, and retype any line containing a mistake.

Now type these sentences:

He quarrelled over the question of his
qualifications.
He had played Harlequin in his quaint costume
at the Questors Theatre.
He was acquainted with the queer questions,
and quit.
Quickly he requested the quarterly quota.
He knew the quotation concerning Quinquireme,
but not that concerning Quietus.

Look at the chart:

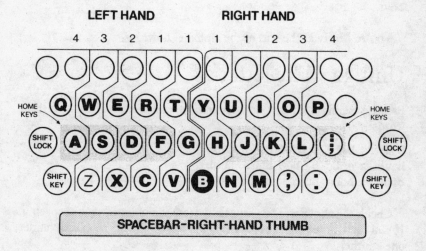

Your new letter is **b**. To type it, you use the first finger of your right hand. Strike the home key **j**. Reach down and well to the left, and strike **b**. Return your finger to its home key immediately. Practise typing:

jhj**b**j jhj**b**j jhj**b**j jhj**b**j jhj**b**j jhj**b**j jhj**b**j

Make sure that your other fingers are on their home keys.
Now type these words:

bob**b**le **Bib**les **b**u**bb**le **b**a**bb**le **b**o**bb**ed
Ben**b**ow da**bb**le ru**bb**er du**bb**ed ru**bb**ed
so**bb**ed ho**bb**le ga**bb**le fi**bb**ed lo**bb**ed

Check to see if you have made any mistakes. Now type these sentences:

Betty **b**ought **b**est **b**utter for **B**elinda.
The **b**rawny **b**owler **b**owled a **b**ouncer to the **b**old **b**atsman.
Brian played the **b**assoon in **B**ootle **B**rass **B**and.
Brass **b**uys **b**read and **b**utter.
Make your **b**ed in **b**racken, not **b**ram**b**les.
Bar**b**ara **b**ustled **b**usily **b**aking **b**atter.
Best **b**randy is a drink for **b**rave men, not for **b**oys.

You're nearly at the end of the alphabet now!

Unit 32 The letter z

Practise typing your last new letter **b** several times. Then type these words:

bul**b**ous **b**a**b**y im**b**i**b**e **b**a**b**el co**bb**le
bau**b**les e**bb**s **b**ar**b**ed **b**lur**b** ho**bb**le
bo**bb**les **b**o**b**s **b**ur**b**le **b**ar**b**s **b**ar**b**er

Check the above words – especially from the point of view of spacing. If you have typed them accurately, the words should be exactly under one another.
Now type these sentences:

The beautiful blackbird broke into a
breathtaking song, from the bare branch.
Bill the bully bragged about his bravery.
The beery bravadoes were brawling at the
Black Bull.
Brenda likes her bread buttered on both sides.
The bride and bridegroom bought the bricabrac
from the boutique on the bridge.

Look at the chart:

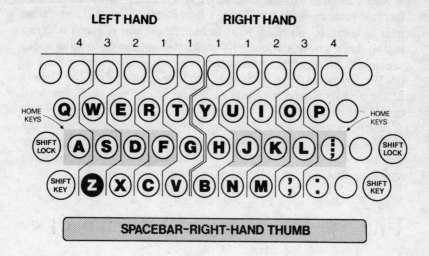

Your new letter is **z**. This is typed with the third finger of the left hand. Strike **s**. Reach down and to the left, and strike **z**. Return your finger to its home key **s** immediately. Now type these words:

zoo size zero zigzag zoom seize assize
zed azure ozone zip zenith zodiac zany
zebra zither zeal zephyr seizure amaze

And now type these sentences:

The crazy zebra zigzagged through the maze.
The New Zealander was amazed at the zither.
The zephyr blew the ozone from the hazy sky and
the azure sea.
The zany man zoomed round the zone in his zoot
suit.
Lazy Hazel was dazed by the size of the task.

Now you have learnt to type all the letters of the alphabet. Type them in order:

abcdefghijklmnopqrstuvwxyz

Don't stop here. Read the next dozen lines *before you go on!*

Now that you have mastered all the letters of the alphabet, you may feel that you can sit back and take a rest. But there are still some more keys to learn. If you really want to become the sort of typist who can just sit down and type whatever you like without having to think about the mechanics of working the typewriter, you still have some more to do. While you are doing it, though, you'll be practising the basic letters of the alphabet. And with any skill (and typing *is* a skill) you need practice to perfect it.

Another reason for not giving up now is that you've just got to the really interesting part. You won't find it nearly so difficult to master new keys now that you've got the hang of things. And you'll find more and more that you are really enjoying using your typewriter.

Unit 33   The basic punctuation marks

You have already learnt to type the **full stop**, the **comma**, the **colon**, and the **semicolon**. Type the following:

out; and: the. his, her; our: yet.
we; to. on: at, by: or. no: of,

When you type the full stop at the end of a sentence, you should normally tap the spacebar twice. After a comma, a semicolon or a colon, you should tap the spacebar once. In this unit, you will once again be reminded by the symbol * how many times you should tap the spacebar.

Apart from marking the end of a sentence, the full stop has several other uses in typewriting; but, first of all, type the following:

A sentence is a complete statement.**At the end
of most sentences, the full stop is typed.**The
spacebar is tapped twice afterwards.

The next sentences show other uses of the full stop. Type them all out:

If you omit something from a quotation*...*you
type three full stops in the middle of a
sentence.**If you omit something from the end of
a sentence, you type four full stops*....

You use the full stop to separate pounds from
pence when you type a sum of money in figures.
You will learn more about this later in this
book.

You use the full stop at the end of some
abbreviations.**But abbreviations like MC and am
are now usually typed without full stops.

The full stop is also used after figures in
numbered paragraphs.**You will learn more about
this when you come to type figures.

The **comma** is probably the most commonly used punctuation mark
there is. Often it is an important part of the meaning of the sentence.
Type the following two sentences:

This author says the reader is a fool.
This author,*says the reader,*is a fool.

Never say commas don't matter!
Commas are also used to separate adjectives (words that describe
nouns), when two or more are used. Type these examples:

He was a miserly,*scrounging,*tightfisted man.
She was a dear old lady.

Why no comma after *dear*? Usually when you can't reverse the
adjectives, you don't need a comma.
The comma is also used to separate short items in a list. Type this:

She bought ham,*gherkins,*salad,*and bread.
He drank two whiskies, *one gin, *and four pints
of beer.

The comma is also used to separate salutations from the main part of
the sentence. Type these sentences:

I should be grateful,*Ruth,*if you would kindly
take your elbow out of my eye.
I hope that you will not mind,*sir,*if I go.

The comma is used to separate descriptive phrases from the main
part of a sentence. Type these:

The woman,*who was well over forty,*said that
girls must stick together.
The shop,*a little shop that sold everything
and knew everyone,*was open until eight.

The comma is also often used in typing numbers containing more
than three figures. You'll learn more about this when you come to learn
to type the figures on the top row of the keyboard.

The **semicolon** marks a stronger break in the sentence than the
comma. It is used in much the same way as the comma, except that it
marks a more definite pause. It is used to separate two complete
sentences that are joined by the words *and* or *but*. Type these examples:

John has wanted to go on the cruise;*but now
that he has jaundice it is impossible.
I have never liked treacle tart;*and I can see
no reason to try to make myself like it now.
He brought with him a teddybear that had lost
an eye in some former nursery war;*five pebbles
that he had gathered on Whitstable beach last
summer;*and a collection of some thirty model
cars that were gifts from a series of
benevolent uncles. Almost as an afterthought,
he brought clothes for the holiday.

The comma may be the most used punctuation mark, but the **colon**
is probably the most misused. It is used to show that something is to
follow – either on the same line, or immediately below. Type these
examples:

She made out her shopping list:*two pairs of
tights; one tee shirt printed with her name
on the front; and a pair of coloured socks.
They were a mixed bunch:*one or two people who had
lived in the block since before the war and who
were still paying minuscule rents; a couple of
postgraduate students who had furnished tenancies;
and a group of staunch middleclass people who had
bought their homes and wanted to stick to them.

The colon is also used to separate two complete sentences that are
connected in sense. Type these examples:

Sausages are fattening:*you should have salad
instead.
Roger is not here:*you will have to phone him.
Get out at the Bank:*Moorgate is quite near.

Notice when you next read your morning newspaper how punctuation marks are used there. And, before you put these sentences away
in your folder, read through them to make sure that you understand
how the different punctuation marks are used.

And, while you're about it, look at the back of your paper. Is your
touch light enough? Or are you puncturing the paper?

Unit 34 The figure 1

Remember from your last unit:

two spaces at the **end** of a sentence
one space after a **comma**, **semicolon** or **colon** in the **middle** of a
sentence

You should be able to remember this for yourself now. You won't be
reminded by signs in this unit. You've been warned!

Look at the chart:

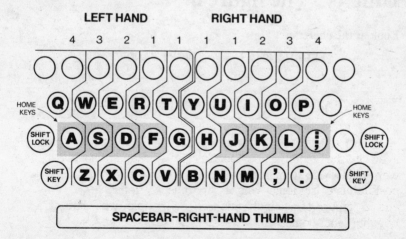

Your new character – the figure **1** – is not shown. On most typewriters
it is on the top row of the keyboard, at the extreme left. Look for it on

your own machine, and mark it in for yourself on the chart. You can see from the chart which finger you have to use to type it. Practise typing it several times, typing first the key immediately above the home key, and then returning your finger to its home key before you make the longer reach to the top row of the keyboard.

If your typewriter hasn't got a key for the figure **1**, you use the small letter **el** (**1**) instead. Type the following:

He was **11** years of age.
Mrs Johnson lived at **1** High Street, London
SE**1** AJ**1**.
There were **111** boxes in the store, and another
11 in the cupboard.
I gave him **1**p change.
The lettuces were **11**p each.
He strode out on to Court No. **1**.
Look at page **1** of this book.
Then look at page **11**.

Check the second sentence against this book. It's easy, when you type postal codes, to forget that most figures have to be typed without using the shift key.

Unit 35   The figure **8**

Look at the chart:

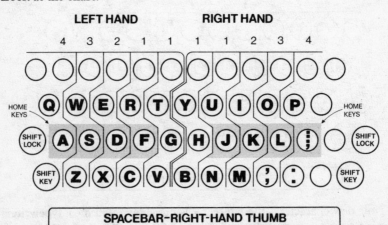

LEFT HAND   RIGHT HAND

4   3   2   1   1   1   1   2   3   4

HOME KEYS   Q W E R T Y U I O P   HOME KEYS

SHIFT LOCK   A S D F G H J K L ;   SHIFT LOCK

SHIFT KEY   Z X C V B N M , .   SHIFT KEY

SPACEBAR–RIGHT-HAND THUMB

Mark the figure **1** on it, which you learnt in your last unit. Now look for and mark in the figure **8**. Study the chart so that you can see which finger you should use. On most typewriters, you use the first finger of your right hand, reaching up from the home key **j**. Check carefully on your own typewriter, though, and practise typing this new figure several times, keeping to this drill:

1. Type the home key.
2. Type the key in the row above it.
3. Type the home key again.
4. Type the figure **8** on the top row of the keyboard.
5. Type the home key again.
6. Make sure that all your other fingers are on their home keys all the time you are doing this.

Now type these sentences:

He was **18** years old.
His mother was pleased because he came 1st in
the race.
She could skate a Figure **8**.
She started work at **8** am.
He was born in 18**8**1.

In the last sentence the number containing four figures has no comma, because the number represents a date. There is also no comma in numbers of four figures when the numbers represent page numbers in a book. But in other numbers of more than three figures commas are often used to separate millions from thousands, and thousands from hundreds. Type these examples:

He was born in 18**1**8.
(no comma because it's a date)

Turn to page 11**88**.
(no comma because it's a page number)

He counted his collection: it numbered 1,118.
The census showed that 1,1**8**1,118 people lived
in the city.

You may notice that in modern commercial and technical writing a space rather than a comma is often used to separate large numbers.

Unit 36 the figure 4

Look at the chart:

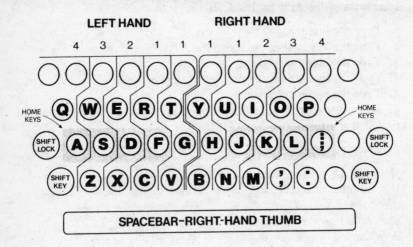

Mark on it the position of the figure **4** on your own typewriter. On most machines, this figure is typed with the second finger of the left hand. Practise striking it. Strike the home key first; then the key immediately above the home key; then the home key again; and then reach up from the home key to the top row.

Now type the following sentences:

Please telephone him on Extension 18**44**.
He served in the **44**th Battalion in the last war.
I am annoyed because you came 1st, and I came **4**th.
The film started at 8 pm.
The tomatoes cost **44**p.

Notice particularly that **you don't type a full stop after 1st, 4th, and contractions like them,** unless, of course, they are at the end of a sentence.

Unit 37   The figure 7

Look at the chart:

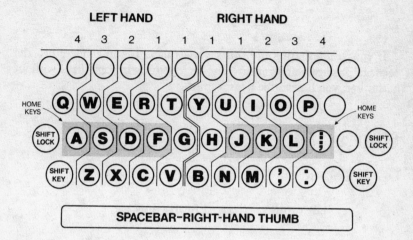

Mark on it the figure **7** as it is placed on your own typewriter. On most typewriters, it is typed with the first finger of the right hand. Practise typing it several times, as you did when you learnt the figure **4**. Remember to keep all your other fingers on their home keys all the time during your practice. Now type these sentences:

I like 4711 Eau de Cologne.
In 1877 Queen Victoria became Empress of India.
The odds are 7 to 1.
Viscount Montgomery was born on 17th November 1887.
It is 477 mm long.
Clive of India died in 1774.

Check very carefully the last two sentences you have typed. Mark in any errors, and re-type any sentence in which there is an error.

Are you still returning the carriage promptly? Keep in good practice by typing all the numbers you have learnt, one under the other like this:

1
8

4
7
1
8
4
7

If you are hesitating, do this several times. If you can't return the carriage promptly and return your fingers to their home keys without hesitating, you'll never be a fast typist.

Unit 38   The figure **2**

Look at the chart:

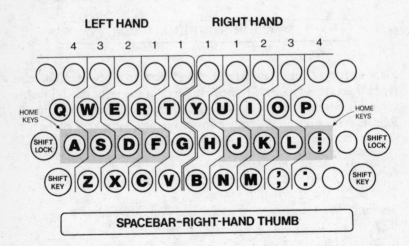

Write in the position of the figure **2** on your chart. Usually it is typed with the third finger of the left hand. Practise typing this figure several times. Remember to keep to this drill:

1. Type the home key.
2. Type the key in the row above it.
3. Type the home key again.
4. Type the figure **2** on the top row of the keyboard.

5. Type the home key again.

6. Make sure that all your other fingers are on their home keys all the time you are doing this.

Now type these sentences:

Grouse shooting starts on 1**2**th August.
At one time in England you reached the age of
majority at **2**1: now you reach it at 18.
The **2**nd wedding anniversary is called the cotton
wedding.
You can hear that on Radio **2**.
Tchaikovsky wrote the 181**2** Overture.
In 181**2** Napoleon retreated from Moscow.
Fig. **2** is on page 1**22**.
The actress came on in Act **2**.

Type all the numbers you know before you go on to the next unit:

1, 8, 4, 7, 2

Unit 39   The figure **9**

Once again, look at the chart:

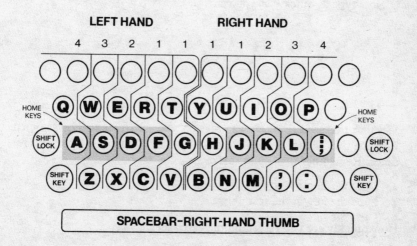

LEFT HAND   RIGHT HAND

4   3   2   1   1   1   1   2   3   4

HOME KEYS   Q W E R T Y U I O P   HOME KEYS
SHIFT LOCK   A S D F G H J K L ;   SHIFT LOCK
SHIFT KEY   Z X C V B N M , .   SHIFT KEY

SPACEBAR—RIGHT-HAND THUMB

Mark in the positions on your typewriter of all the figures you have learnt so far. Now mark in the position of the figure **9**. On most machines, it is typed with the second finger of the right hand. Practise typing it in the usual way, reaching up from the home key to the key in the row immediately above it, returning your finger to its home key, and then reaching up and striking the figure key on the top row.

Now type these sentences:

Dial **999** for police, fire or ambulance.
Take the figure **9**. Multiply it by any number.
Add together the digits of the resulting number.
Their total will always be a multiple of **9**. As an
example, multiply **9** by **9**. The result is 81. Add
together 8 and 1. The total is **9**. Multiply **9** by 8.
The result is 72. Add together 7 and 2. The total
is **9**.
The first world war ended in 19 18.
The Queen was married in 1947.
29th June is the feast of St Peter and St Paul.
Any number of which the digits add up to a
multiple of **9** can be divided by **9**. Take 18**9**. The
digits add up to 18.
So 18**9** can be divided by **9**. Try the
same procedure with the number **199,999,99**8. Then
try it with any number you like to think of.

Now type as quickly as you can:

1
8
7
2
9
4
1
8
7
2
9
4

How quickly are you returning the carriage?

Unit 40   The figure **5**

On nearly all typewriters the figure **5** is typed with the first finger of the left hand. Look at the chart:

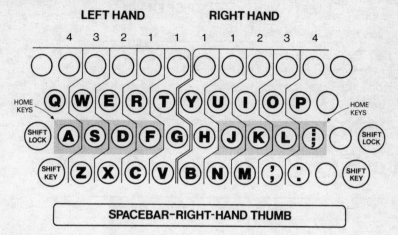

LEFT HAND   **RIGHT HAND**

SPACEBAR–RIGHT-HAND THUMB

Mark on it the positions of all the numbers you have so far learnt to type. Then add the figure 5. Practise typing this several times. Check that all your other fingers are on their home keys while you are typing this figure. Now practise this new figure still further by typing these sentences:

Any number that ends with a **5** or a zero can be
divided exactly by **5**. Type **5**1**5**,2**85** to try this.
The 2**5**th wedding anniversary is called a silver
wedding.
Please to remember the **5**th of November,
With gunpowder, treason and plot.
There are **5**2 cards in an ordinary pack of
playing cards, not counting the jokers.
In 18**5**1, the Great Exhibition took place in
London.

Check the last two sentences that you have typed. If you have made any mistakes in them type them a second time.

Are you still keeping your typed sheets in your folder? Look back through them. You can see how much progress you have made.

Unit 41 The figure **0**

Look at the chart:

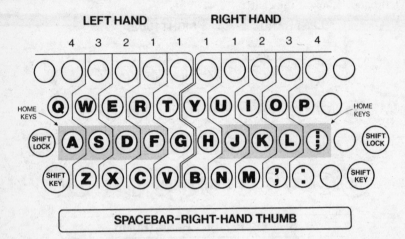

Mark on it the positions of all the figures you have already learnt. Then mark in the figure **0**. On some typewriters, it is on the top row of the keyboard next to the figure **9**, in which case it is typed with the third finger of the right hand. On some typewriters there is no key for **0**. Instead, you use the shift key to type a capital letter **O**. If there is no key for the figure **0** on your typewriter, circle the letter **O** on your chart, so that it reminds you which key to use for this figure.

Practise typing **0** several times, before you start the following exercises:

The birthday of Prince Edward is 1**0**th March.
He was driving a Morris 1**000**.
However glamorous he may have appeared, **00**7 was
probably very uncomfortable to live with.
The square root of 1**00** is 1**0**, and of 1,**000,000**,
1,**000**.
If you stand at a height of 1,**000** feet, the
horizon is over 41 miles away.
I start work at 9 am and finish at 5 pm; or, if
you use the international clock, I start at **0900**
hours, and finish at 17**00** hours.

Type the following as quickly as you can before you go on to the next unit:

18472950   12457890

Are you still setting your margin stops at **30** and **80**?

Unit 42   The figure **6**

Look at the chart:

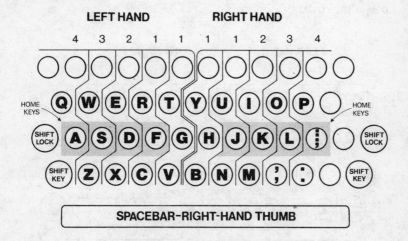

Mark in all the figures you have learnt so far. Look for the figure **6**. Mark it on the chart. On most typewriters it is typed with the first finger of the left hand. To type it you have to reach over to the right when you reach up to the top row.

Practise typing this key several times before you start to type these sentences:

In 174**6**, the English defeated the Scots at
Culloden.
In 1**66**5, The Great Plague spread through London.

In 1**666**, the Great Fire of London helped to
clear the slums that had caused the epidemic to
spread so quickly.
In 1**066**, William the Conqueror defeated Harold
at the Battle of Hastings.
He caught the 1**6**1**6** train to Brighton. It was
6 minutes late starting, and 1**6** minutes late
arriving.

Unit 43   The figure **3**

Look at the chart:

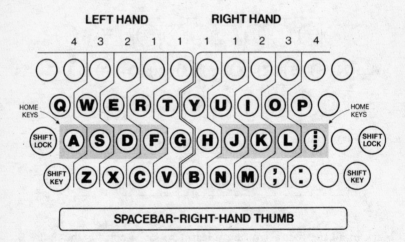

Mark on it all the figures you have already learnt. Then mark in the key
for the figure **3**. Usually, it's typed with the third finger of the left hand.
Practise typing it several times, making sure that you keep all your
other fingers on their home keys.

Now type these sentences:

It is an old superstition that number 1**3**
is unlucky.

Friday the 13th is thought to be even more unlucky.

On 3rd September, 1939, Great Britain declared war on Germany.

January has 31 days; so has December.

You can hear it all on Radio 3.

Unit 43 teaches you to type the figure 3.

Now that you can type the figure 3, you can type all the figures. Type this slowly and rhythmically:

123 456 789 098 076 032 021

Repeat this line twice before you go on to your next unit.

Unit 44 The question mark (?)

Look at the chart:

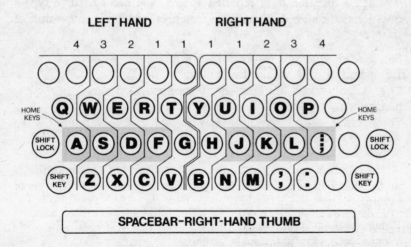

Mark on it all the figures you have learnt. Then look at the keyboard of your typewriter and find the **question mark** (?). Mark this in, too. Its position varies on different typewriters. On some machines, it is on the same key as the **comma**, on the bottom row. On other machines, it is on the top row. When you have marked it in, look carefully at the chart to see which finger you should use to type it. Then practise typing it several times, returning your finger to its home key after each **?**.

You type a question mark at the end of any question that requires an answer. Type these examples:

Why is 13 an unlucky number**?**
My God, my God, why hast thou forsaken me**?**
What colour is it**?**
Why has he gone out**?**
What book are you reading**?**
How fast can you type**?**
When will you come**?**
What has happened to Jock**?**
What do you call your dog**?**
How did you shrink your jeans**?**

Usually the question mark comes at the end of a sentence. **At the end of a sentence**, whether it ends with a full stop, an exclamation mark, or a question mark, **you tap the spacebar twice**.

When a question is in reported speech, you don't need to type a question mark after it. Type these sentences, which are an example of this:

She asked whether he had heard the bell.
He asked if she would be willing to go.
The doctor asked the patient if she had had any
headaches.
The mother asked the little boy to tell her
where he had hidden it.

The question mark is also unnecessary at the end of a sentence that is in the form of a question, but is really a command. Type these examples:

Would you step this way, please.
Would you see that this is attended to quickly.
Would you take some letters.

Before you go on to the next unit, type this line three times, as quickly as you can:

123456789**?** 123456789**?** 123456789**?**

Then type it once, without bothering to be quick. Look at this last line. Mark on it any errors you have made.

Put the sheet in your folder.

Unit 45 The apostrophe (')

Look at the chart:

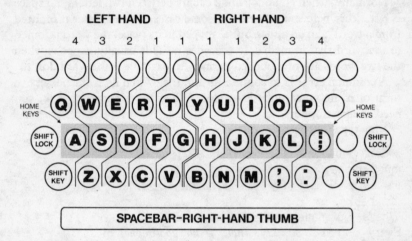

Mark in the numbers you have already learnt, and also the question mark. Now mark in the key for the **apostrophe** ('). On most typewriters it is the shift-key character for the figure **8**. Look at the fingering on your chart. Practise typing the **apostrophe** several times.

The chief use of this key is to show that something has been omitted. It's difficult in some cases to work out where apostrophes go, and also to work out why they go in certain places and not others. The possessive forms of most nouns need an apostrophe – but what is omitted is an "e" which is no longer used anyway. The rule about the apostrophe and possessive nouns is:

Add **'s** to the **singular** form of nouns.

Add **only** the ' to plural forms ending in **s**.
Add **'s** to other plurals.

If this sounds complicated, look at (and type!) the following sentences:

The boy had a red shirt. (*one boy, one shirt*)
The boy's red shirt. (*possessive form – one boy, one shirt*)
The boys had red shirts. (*several boys, several shirts*)
The boys' red shirts. (*possessive form – several boys, several shirts*)
The man's hat. (*one man, one hat*)
The men's hats. (*several men, several hats*)

Normally, when an **apostrophe** occurs between two letters, no space is left either before or after it. In some cases, when a letter is omitted from a word, and an **apostrophe** is typed in its place, the word is joined to the word that immediately precedes it. This usually happens when the two words are pronounced as one. An example is the word **don't**.

A common error is to confuse **its** and **it's**. When **its** is the possessive form of **it**, no apostrophe is needed. When **it's** is short for **it is**, you need an apostrophe.

Now type these sentences:

I don't think I can help, because I haven't
much money.
It's early closing day, and I haven't been to
the bank.
What's the matter with the boy's bike?
Every dog has its day. (*note – no apostrophe*)
Gerald O'Connor called at eleven o'clock.
I don't think I'd like to do that.
It's one of the great tragedies of my life that
I can't sing in tune.
That's no lady, that's my wife.

Before you go on to Unit 46, type these sentences, putting in the apostrophes where you think they are necessary:

Its not easy to find a small boys bicycle
when you dont know where hes left it.
I dont think it can have been stolen as its
chain was loose.

Michael hadnt the courage to tell his father
hed lost it.
His father wouldnt have been very pleased.
Thats an understatement.

Check what you have typed. Turn this book upside down to do this:

That's an understatement.
His father wouldn't have been very pleased.
he'd lost it.
Michael hadn't the courage to tell his father
chain was loose.
I don't think it can have been stolen as its
when you don't know where he's left it.
It's not easy to find a small boy's bicycle

If you've made any mistakes over the apostrophe, read this unit through again.

Unit 46   The backspacer

The key for the **backspacer** isn't a character key. It's a gadget on the typewriter that makes the typewriter operate in a certain way – much as the spacebar does. But, whilst tapping the spacebar makes the roller move from right to left so that a space is left, the **backspacer** makes the roller move from left to right – so that you're back to the last thing you typed.

This key is on different places on different typewriters. It is often marked with an arrow, and is either at the left or the right of the alphabet keys. Find out where it is on your typewriter.

To operate it, you have to press it right down. It's the same touch that you use to operate the shift key or shift lock. When you have found the key for the **backspacer** on your own typewriter, practise operating it with your little finger. With your other fingers on their home keys, practise working it several times, returning your little finger to its home key after each striking.

In the next few units, you'll see how you use this gadget in conjunction with different keys on the top row of the keyboard.

Before you go on to the next unit, type these sentences. You should now be able to type them without hesitating:

In London, 2,000 people sleep in the open
each night; but there are 100,000 empty homes.
The Battle of Culloden took place in 1746.
You can see Cumberland's Stone at Culloden.
1929 was a great year for Red Burgundy.
3 and 7 are prime numbers.
There's not so much difference now between men's
and women's clothes.
Mind your p's and q's.

Check the last sentence only – how's your typing?

Unit 47   The exclamation mark (!)

Look at the chart:

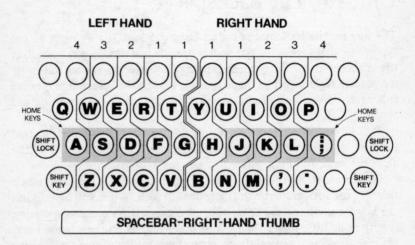

Mark on it all the figures and other extra characters you have learnt. Look to find out where the **exclamation mark** (!) is on your typewriter. Mark it on the chart, too.

If your typewriter has no key for the exclamation mark, you can type it by using the key for the apostrophe and the full stop – and – yes! – the backspacer. To do this:

1. Depress the shift key.
2. Type the apostrophe.
3. Release the shift key.
4. Backspace once.
5. Type the full stop.

Whether or not you have a key for the **exclamation mark** on your typewriter, practise typing this punctuation mark several times. Watch that you are using the correct finger for this. Practise keeping the rest of your fingers on their home keys.

The **exclamation mark** is, as its name suggests, used to express surprise, command, astonishment. It's usually typed at the end of a sentence. No space is needed before you type it. But, like any other punctuation mark, it needs two spaces after it when it appears at the end of a sentence.

Type the following:

Stop!
Fire!
Help!
Never!
No!
Danger!
Shut up!
Get out!
Get lost!
Halt!
Quiet!
Present arms!
Attention!
Good!
Cut!
Scram!
Let!
Fault!

This exercise gives you extra practice in returning the carriage quickly. Are you still returning it swiftly and putting your fingers back on to their home keys without hesitation? If you're not, type the exercise again, paying particular attention to this.

Unit 48 The solidus (/)

Look at the chart:

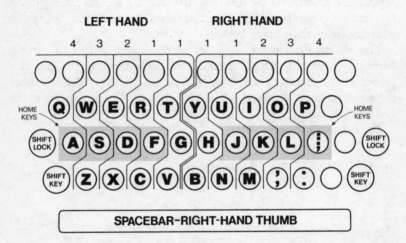

Mark in the **solidus** (/). On most typewriters this key is the shift-key character for the figure **3**. Practise typing it several times, returning your finger to its home key after each typing.

The **solidus** isn't one of the most widely used keys. Its chief use is to separate alternatives. In the following sentences you will see how it is used. Type them all:

Bring with you your suitcase and/or rucksack.
I should like a single/double/twinbedded room.
Please send me a small/medium/large size.

If you have to help with running a club in your evenings, you'll find you use the **solidus** on duplicated forms when members have to make a choice.

Now type this passage as quickly as you can:

It's easy to learn to type as long as you
remember one thing. It's much more important
to practise for 15 minutes each day than for two
hours a week. It's constant regular practice
that makes a skilled typist.

Now type the paragraph at your normal rate. Read it through, and
mark in any errors. Put it in your folder. Are you still remembering to
date your work?

Unit 49 The dash (-)

Look at the chart:

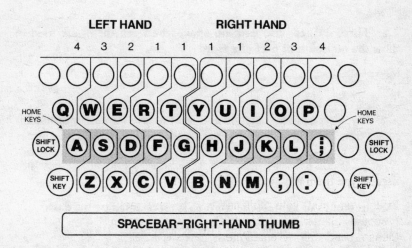

Fill in the extra characters that you have learnt so far. Now fill in the
key for the dash (-). It will usually be found on the top row of the

keyboard towards the right-hand side. Don't confuse it with the character over the figure **6**, which you will be learning later.

Practise typing the dash (-) several times. You can see from your chart which finger you should use.

This character on the typewriter has two different functions. It's both a **dash** and a **hyphen**. As a **dash**, it is used as a punctuation mark to show an addition or interruption to a sentence. Type these examples, leaving a **space before and after each dash**. The symbol * is to remind you:

The boy*-*he was obviously lying*-*said that he
hadn't been near the orchard.
The book*-*several publishers had turned it
down*-*became a bestseller.

The dash has several other uses. Read this list of them, and type out all the examples:

1. Three **dashes**, with **no spaces between them**, are used to indicate an **interruption** in speech (useful if you're typing your own best-selling novel!):

I've had enough! I'm jumping---
Stop!

2. Three **dashes**, also with **no spaces between them**, are used to show the **omission of part of a word**

Mr B---n
D---!

3. If you type out a quotation and want to give the author or book it comes from, you use a **dash** to **separate the quotation from its source**:

To every thing there is a season, and a time to
every purpose under heaven. *-*Ecclesiastes

4. In groups of figures, the word **to** is represented by the **dash**:

The 1914-18 war ended on 11th November, 1918.
The index is on pages 517-18

5. The **dash** is sometimes used with the **colon** when what follows is on a separate line.

6. The dash is used as a **hyphen**. In this case, it has **no space before or after it**.

Some compound words need a hyphen in the middle. If you're in doubt about whether or not a word has a hyphen, check it in a dictionary.

Words in which two vowels that are sounded separately come one after the other sometimes have a hyphen:

co-ordinate; co-operate; co-opt; co-eternal

7. A **hyphen** is needed in composite adjectives. There's a good deal of difference, if you think about it, between a pickled-herring merchant, and a pickled herring-merchant. Type all these sentences, which give plenty of examples of composite adjectives:

It was a never-to-be-forgotten event.
He spoke in a matter-of-fact tone.
She had beautiful blue-grey eyes.
It was a last-minute decision.

8. The **hyphen** is also used to **divide words at the ends of lines**. You will find that you have to do this in typewriting when a long word comes towards the end of a line. In the next unit, I'll show you how this is done.

Unit 50   Margins

So far all the exercises you have been asked to type have been designed so that they can be typed with margins of **30** at the left-hand side and **80** at the right-hand side. Obviously, you won't always want to have these margins, and obviously you'll often have to type things where you can't follow the lines exactly.

In Unit 2, I showed you how to set the margin stops. Re-read this unit (page 13). By moving the margin stops, you can vary the margins as you like.

If your typewriter is fitted with **elite** type, there are **12** characters or spaces to the inch. If it is fitted with **pica** type, there are **10** characters or spaces to the inch.

If your paper is A4, it is 8¼ **inches wide,** or **210 mm**. It's a matter of simple arithmetic then to work out that, on A4 paper, you can type **82** characters in **pica** type, or **99** characters in **elite** type.

To set margins of an inch on each side, you set the stops at:

10 and **72** (**pica,** A4 paper)
12 and **87** (**elite,** A4 paper)

Once you have grasped the simple calculations involved, you can set the margin stops for any width of margin you like.

Life (or rather typing) would be all very simple if everything you typed were set so that you could type it line for line.

If you see a piece from a newspaper that you want to copy out and keep, the margins will be completely different from yours. What you have to do is to listen for the **warning bell** that automatically rings on your typewriter when you're approaching the end of a line. On most typewriters, it rings four spaces before you reach the right-hand margin stop. Check how many spaces it is before the margin on your own typewriter. You can do this easily by tapping the spacebar until you hear the bell ring. Then go on tapping the spacebar, and counting the number of times you tap it before you reach the right-hand margin stop and can go no farther. You will then know how many characters you can type after the bell rings and before you reach your right-hand margin.

So, when you're typing and the bell rings, you can type only a very short new word – or you can finish the one you're typing provided it isn't too long. If it is, you have to divide it with a hyphen, continuing the rest of the word on the next line. You type a hyphen at the end of the line (with no space before it), and then type the rest of the word at the beginning of the next line. There's no need to type a second hyphen.

You shouldn't divide your word just anywhere. If you do, it will be difficult for the person reading. Ideally you should divide words so that the division doesn't affect the way the word is pronounced. This means that you shouldn't divide words that have only one syllable. Good places to divide are usually between syllables. If you find that you need just one more space to finish a long word before the right-hand margin, you can use the **margin-release key**. Look for this on your typewriter. It's usually on the right-hand side of the keyboard, and it's often marked by arrows going in both directions. When you push it down, you can move the roller past the margin stops on both sides. To work it, you need to make a definite pushing movement with your little finger and hold the key down while you type past the margin stop. Once you've passed the margin stop you can release the key, and go on typing in the margin if you want to. Try not to use the margin release in this way too much, though – if you do, your right-hand margin will look very uneven.

Now type these words, putting in a hyphen in the places where you would separate them if you had to divide them at the end of a line:

getting spending singing happiness railway
margin paragraph question apostrophe
semicolon typewriter useless punishment

Turn the book upside down to check that you've got the right idea:

get-ting spend-ing sing-ing hap-pi-ness rail-way
mar-gin para-graph ques-tion apos-trophe
semi-colon type-writer use-less pun-ish-ment

Unit 51 Quotation marks (")

Look at the chart:

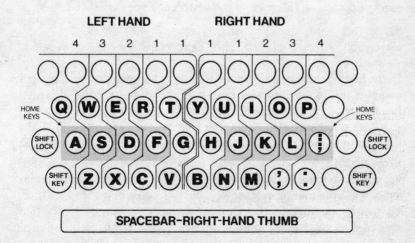

Mark in the punctuation marks and shift-key characters you have already learnt. Now mark in the key for the quotation mark ("). This sign is usually the shift-key character for the figure 2. You can check with the chart which finger you should use to type it. Practise typing it several times, returning your finger to its home key after each typing.

You should type **quotation marks** (") at the **beginning** and **end** of anything you quote. What you quote may be either a passage from literature or what someone says. The same character is used for both the opening and closing of the quotation. Type these examples, setting your margin stops at **35** and **80**. You'll have to listen for the warning bell and divide words at the end of the line when necessary:

Queen Elizabeth I of England said on her death-bed that she would give "all my possessions for a moment of time". He shouted at her: "I don't want to be done good to!"

If you type out a quotation of several paragraphs, the **quotation marks** appear at the **beginning** of **each** paragraph, and at the end of the **last** one.

If you have to type a **quotation within a quotation**, you use **single** quotation marks **within double** ones. For the single ones, you use the key for the apostrophe. Type this example:

"Have you read 'Alternative London'?" he asked.

The position of **quotation marks** in relation to other punctuation marks depends on the sense of the sentence. Type these two sentences:

"What on earth are you talking about?" he asked.
Have you a copy of "To The Lighthouse"?

In the first one, the question mark definitely **belongs** to what is quoted, and goes **inside the quotation marks**. In the second, the question mark is not part of the quoted matter, and is typed outside the quotes.

If you're writing something that involves speech, you may find it difficult to know where to put the **quotation marks** in relation to other punctuation marks. Type out these sentences:

"I hate you!" he shouted.
"The compliment is reciprocated", she retorted.
"Where", he asked, "is the key to the safe?"
"I'm not telling you", she said. "It's been hidden."

In the first two sentences, the punctuation is fairly straightforward. In both cases, a complete quoted sentence is followed by **he shouted** or **she retorted**. The main thing to notice about these two examples is that although they are complete sentences no full stop is typed at the end of them. In the case of the first, the sentence ends with an exclamation mark. This is retained – and so would a question mark be. But a full stop is replaced by a comma when it would have occurred immediately before a phrase like **she said, she answered,** or **she retorted**.

In the second two examples, the words **he asked** and **she said** are in the middle of what is said instead of at the end. In the first line, **he asked** is in the middle of one complete sentence, and is therefore "comma-ed" off. In the second example, **she said** is between quoted sentences. So a comma is typed before **she said**, but a full stop after it. And the second sentence **It's been hidden** starts with a capital letter because it's a new sentence. In these examples, you'll notice that a fresh line is started for each person speaking. This is common practice.

Quotation marks aren't needed when the speech is reported. Type these two examples:

He asked where the key to the safe was.
She said that she wasn't going to tell him.

You may sometimes want to type out a quotation, but to omit something from it. The recognized way to do this is to type three full stops if you miss out something from the middle, or four full stops if you miss out something from the end. Type out these examples:

"The human species ... is composed of two distinct races, the men who borrow and the men who lend." - Charles Lamb
"I never read a book before reviewing it ...."
- The Rev. Sydney Smith

You can also use quotation marks for nicknames, for book titles and for slang expressions. Type out these examples:

It wasn't for nothing that he was known as "The Basher of Bethnal Green".
She was sitting happily reading "Winnie-The-Pooh".
What, asked the judge, did the young man mean when he said he wasn't "into" that?

Now type all the numbers, one under the other like this:

1
2
3
4
5
6
7
8
9
0

You should now be able to type them without hesitating.

Before you put these sheets in your folder, look at your right-hand margin. Are you remembering to divide words when the warning bell rings?

Are you still dating your work? Look back through your folder. You can see how much progress you have made.

Unit 52   The brackets (())

Before you start work on this unit, re-read the last unit on quotation marks to make sure that you remember all the points made.

Now look at the chart:

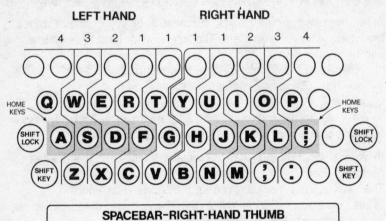

Mark on it the figures and extra characters you have already learnt. Now mark on it the keys for the brackets (**()**). They are usually on the top row of the keyboard at the right-hand side. Practise typing them several times, returning your fingers to their home keys between typings.

Now type this line twice:

1234567890.,;"/'-**()**

You should be able to type it without looking at the keyboard, although, because of the large number of top-row characters and of shift-key characters, you won't be able to get up a high speed.

The chief use of the two **brackets** (left-hand and right-hand) is to separate from the main part of a sentence words that are an aside, an addition, or an explanation. You don't need to leave a space after the opening (left-hand) bracket, or before the closing (right-hand) one. Type these examples:

She **(**Tessa**)** came into the room.
The manager **(**Mr Tracey**)** opened the drawer of his desk very deliberately.

You can use brackets to express surprise or doubt by typing an exclamation mark or a question mark inside them in the middle of a sentence. Type these two examples:

The butler **(**!**)** showed us in.
His secretary **(**?**)** told us he was not at home.

Brackets are often used in the numbering of paragraphs if you have to type a report. In this case, make sure that the numbers range on the right-hand side, and not on the left. Type the following – it will give you good practice in returning the carriage:

(1)
(2)
(3)
(4)
(5)
(6)
(7)
(8)

(9)
(10)

Did you find it easy to return the carriage and put the fingers of your left hand back on the home keys without hesitation?

Where you put punctuation marks in relation to brackets depends on the sense of the sentence. The rules are the same as with quotation marks. When the punctuation marks belong to what is inside the brackets, they are typed inside the brackets. Otherwise they are not. Type these two examples:

He offered to buy her a drink (an unheard-of happening).
(It was an unheard-of happening.)

In the first sentence, the words in brackets are part of the main sentence, and the full stop marking the end of the sentence is typed outside the closing bracket. In the second sentence, the whole sentence is inside the brackets, and the full stop belongs with the sentence, inside the closing brackets.

You can also use the brackets to make a long brace if, for example, you have to type a form for a club you belong to. Type out this example:

(single room with own bath
(single room
(double room with own bath
I should like   (double room
(twin-bedded room with own bath
(twin-bedded room
(dormitory accommodation

Cross out whatever does not apply.

To type this you'll find it easiest to set your left-hand margin stop for the middle of the sheet of paper. Then type the brackets and the words after them. Then re-set the left-hand margin stop, and type in the words **I should like**.

How are you managing with your right-hand margin? Re-read the unit on margins on page 93.

Unit 53 The underscore and the ribbon lever

Look at the chart:

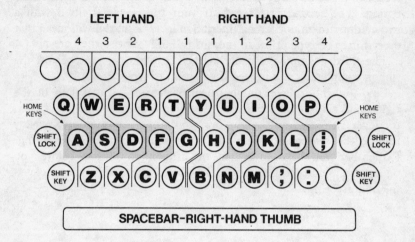

Mark in all the numbers and extra characters you already know. Then mark in the key for the **underscore**. It is usually the shift-key character for the figure **6**. Practise typing it several times, returning the finger to its home key after each typing.

The function of this key is to print an underlining under another character. If the underlining is a long one, you can move the carriage back, push down the shift lock, and type the **underscore**. To move the carriage back to do this, don't use the carriage-return lever as it will move the paper up a space. Use instead the right-hand knob of the roller. If the underscoring is a short one, it's simpler to use the back-spacer, moving the carriage back one space at a time.

The chief use of the **underscore** is to emphasize important words, including headings. Type out these sentences. For short **underscores**, use the backspacer. For long ones, use the roller knob to move the roller back. Keep your margin stops at **35** and **80**.

He said he was <u>not</u> going.

She said she wouldn't go <u>even if she were paid to do so.</u>

Her name is <u>Dianne</u>, not <u>Diana.</u>

If you write for tickets, you can get them <u>free of charge</u>.

Repeat these sentences, using a **red** underscore.

You can make your underscoring even more emphatic if you do it in red. On your typewriter, you'll find a **ribbon lever**. It's usually marked for three positions. One is for black, which is the normal position for typing. The second is for red. If your typewriter is fitted with a two-colour ribbon, switching the ribbon lever on to **red** will mean that everything you type prints in **red**, instead of black.

The third position is usually marked in white. It switches off the ribbon completely, and is used if you want to type stencils.

Find the **ribbon lever** on your own typewriter – it is usually on the right-hand side of the keyboard. If your ribbon is two-colour, switch the lever on to **red** and type a few words to see how it works. Now re-type the sentences, using the **red** ribbon for the underscoring. Remember you have to switch the ribbon on to **red** before you underscore; and then switch it back to black after you have completed the underscoring.

Unit 54   The tabulator, paragraphs, and the variable line spacer

Look at your typewriter and see whether you can find on it the **tabulator** mechanism. This usually consists of a **tabulator set key** (marked +), and a tabulator release key (marked −). These two keys together with a **tabulator key** (check where it is on your keyboard) make it possible for you to move the roller quickly to a position that you decide on in advance. This is especially useful if you want to type columns.

To set the **tabulator**, you move the roller to the point at which you want the column to begin. You press the **tabulator set key** (marked +). Then each time you want to type something in this column, you've only to press the **tabulator key** and the roller will automatically move to the point on which you've decided for the column.

Not all typewriters are fitted with a **tabulator** mechanism. Some small typewriters don't have one at all. Others have a simplified kind called a **pre-set mechanism**. With this, you can move the roller only to a limited number of pre-set positions. It's still useful if you have to type columns, but not so useful as a full **tabulator** mechanism.

Another use for the **tabulator** is if you want to indent (that is, set farther in from the margin) the first lines of paragraphs. You don't have to do this. There are three different ways of typing paragraphs. The first is the **indented** method. Type out this example. Set your margin stops for **30 and 80**, and your **tabulator** for **35** on the scale.

A new paragraph is needed whenever a new
subject is started. Very long paragraphs make
a passage difficult to read. Very short paragraphs make a passage read jerkily.

Up to now, you've been typing in **single-line spacing**. If you type paragraphs in **single-line spacing**, you need to leave an **extra line space between paragraphs**.

If you're typing in single-line spacing, and want to leave a double-line space between paragraphs, you return the roller to the left-hand margin point, and then move the carriage-return lever a second time, so that it turns up an extra line space. If you're typing an **indented** paragraph, you press the **tabulator key** after you've turned up this extra line space. When you use the tabulator mechanism, it's important to press the key down very firmly, and hold it down until the roller comes to rest at the stop.

You can also type paragraphs in **block** form, with no indentation. In this case, you type all lines at the left-hand margin point. The **block** paragraph is usually typed in single-line spacing, with an extra space between paragraphs.

Lastly, there is the **hanging** paragraph. You type the first line at the left-hand margin point, and indent all the others by using your tabulator. Type this example. Set the margin stops at **30 and 80**, and the **tabulator stop** at **35**.

A new paragraph is needed whenever a new
subject is started. Very long paragraphs make
a passage difficult to read. Very short paragraphs make a passage read jerkily.

Most **hanging** paragraphs are typed in single spacing, with a double space between paragraphs.

Single spacing is usually used for writing letters.

Double spacing is usually used for the typing of copy for the printer or for any forms that people have to fill in by hand, as it gives more space for their handwriting.

Treble spacing isn't used very often, but it's handy if you want to type something as a draft as it gives you plenty of room to make handwritten alterations before you type the final version.

To change the line spacing, you have only to move the line-space selector to a new position. You can also vary the line spacing by operating the **variable line spacer**, which frees the line-spacing mechanism. Find this on your own typewriter – the most usual place for it is on the left-hand roller knob. It's a useful gadget if you want to type on a form where the lines don't match those on your typewriter.

If you use the **variable line spacer**, though, you won't get back automatically to the original typing line. If you want to do this, you must use the **line finder** – a small lever which you pull forward. Find this on your typewriter. It's usually near the left-hand end of the roller.

To change the tabulator point (unless you have a pre-set tabulator, in which case you can't change the points) you press the **tabulator key** so that the roller moves to the point where you have set the tabulator. Then you press the **tabulator release key** (marked −). Then you start again fixing the tabulator points where you want them.

Before you go on to the next unit, set your margin stops at **35** and **80**, and a tabulator stop at **40**. Now type these numbers, one under the other, returning the roller after each one, and using the tabulator stop to move the roller into position for typing the numbers:

1
2
3
4
5
6
7
8
9

Leave the margin stops and the tabulator stop in the same position and type the following:

"

```
/
'
(
)
?
!

.
:

,
;
```

Are you operating the tabulator without difficulty? If you're having any trouble at all, do these two exercises again, using double line spacing.

Unit 55   Centring

There are several ways of typing headings. One is to type the heading at the left-hand margin point, like this:

Centring

Underscoring the heading is quick and easy to do, because you've only to move the roller back to the left-hand margin point, depress the shift lock, and work the underscore.

You can vary this by underscoring in red.

Another method of typing headings is to **centre** them. If you're typing with equal left- and right-handed margins, this is easy. Take the width of the sheet of paper in characters:

A4 has **82 pica** characters or **99 elite** characters.

Deduct from this number the number of characters and spaces in the heading you want to centre. Divide this number by two. This is the point on the scale at which you start typing your heading if you want to centre it on the page.

Another simple method of centring is to move the roller so that the typing point is at the centre of the page. Then **backspace once** for every **two** characters in the heading. Then type the heading.

Practise typing centred headings by centring the following on whichever size paper you are using:

London belongs to us!
Tomorrow has been cancelled
Homes not Roads
Stop the world and let me get off
Not right, not left, but forward
The search for identity
Black Sunday
In defence of human beings
Gin and kippers
The hope that died

Notice that, although the first heading has an exclamation mark at the end, none of them has a full stop. Headings don't need a full stop at the end of them. Sometimes they need a question mark if the sense demands it.

For extra practice, choose three more headings from your daily paper, and centre these on a sheet of paper. Check that the headings you have typed are really in the centre of the page.

Don't forget to date your work, and keep it in your folder.

Advance warning! In Unit 58, you'll need carbon paper. If you don't have any, buy a packet from your local stationer's. Buy it the same size as the typing paper you use. At the same time, buy a typing rubber or a packet of chemical eraser strips. If you use a rubber, an eraser shield is also useful. You'll be shown how to use it later.

Unit 56 The ampersand (&) and sums of money

Type the following line twice. Take your time over it. It's more difficult, and needs more concentration than typing words:

1234567890"/_'(),?.:;-

Now look at the chart:

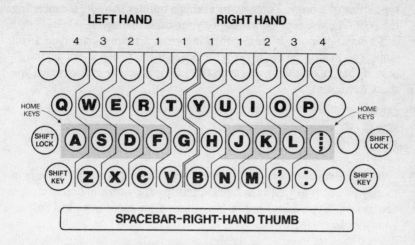

Mark on it all the characters in the exercise you have just typed. Now find and mark in these new characters:

& @ £

All of them are on the top row of the keyboard, and all of them are shift-key characters. Practise typing them several times – you can see from the chart which fingers to use.

Of these new characters, the **ampersand** is seldom used except in the names of firms. Type these examples:

Ackles **&** Pollock Ltd
Pickles **&** Wallop Ltd
Wackles **&** Pollop Ltd

The sign for **at** (@) is used only in invoices and in quoting sums of money. Type these examples, centring them on the page:

54 @ 7p
33 @ 8p
47 @ 4p
52 @ 3p

The £ sign is more important. You're almost certain to want to use it. If you use your typewriter for your own letters, you'll need at times to type sums of money. You may be asking a builder to quote for mending the roof – or you may be writing to your bank manager.

To separate pounds from pence in sums of money, you type a full stop. You *don't* type the letter **p** for pence if the pence follow pounds -- only if they're on their own, as in the example you've just typed. Type these examples:

£15.64
£22.45
£67.82

If a large sum of money is involved, it's a good idea to type the sum of money in words as well as in figures, putting the words in brackets after the figures. Type this example. Set your margin stops at **30** and **80**, and your tabulator stop at **35**:

I accept your quotation of £678.23 (six hundred and seventy-eight pounds and twenty-three pence) for the installation of central heating.

If you ever have to type sums of American money, you can make up a dollar sign by typing a capital **S**, backspacing, and then typing the solidus (/). Type these examples, centring them on the sheet of paper:

$74
$38
$46

Unit 57   Mathematical symbols

If you look at your typewriter, you will see quite a few fractions. The most common ones on the keyboard are:

$\frac{1}{4}$ $\frac{3}{4}$ $\frac{1}{8}$ $\frac{3}{8}$ $\frac{5}{8}$ $\frac{7}{8}$ $\frac{1}{2}$

Look at your keyboard to see whether you can find any others. Type all the fractions on your own keyboard once. Unless the kind of typing you're going to do involves the use of a lot of fractions, you don't really need to learn how to type them. If you feel that it's important for you to learn them, mark them on the chart:

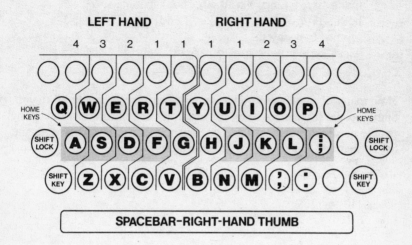

You can see from the chart which fingers to use, and you can practise typing them. The most commonly used fraction is the ½.

There are various other mathematical symbols. These are some of the most common ones. Type them out and keep this list in your folder. Set your margin stops at **30** and **80**, and your tabulator stop at **35**.

+   There is usually a key for this character
    on the keyboard - often on the top row,
    extreme left. If there's no key for
    this character, you have to write it
    in by hand.

=   There is usually a key for this on the
    typewriter. If there isn't, you can make
    this character by typing a **dash**, back-
    spacing, using the line-finder to move
    the roller slightly, and then typing the
    dash again, placing the second one
    slightly under the first one.

-   For the minus sign, you use the **dash**.

×   For the multiplication sign, you use the small letter **x**.

÷   Not many typewriters are equipped with a separate division sign. It is easily made by typing the **dash**, backspacing, holding down the shift key, and then typing the **colon**.

%   Most typewriters are equipped with a sign for this.

How many of these signs you learn to touch-type is largely up to you. Some people (maths teachers, for example) use them a lot. But many people hardly use them at all. Type out the following (margins **30** and **80**) so that you can see how these characters are used:

15 + 45 = 60
33 - 11 = 22
15 × 10 = 150
5% of 150 = $7\frac{1}{2}$
27 ÷ 9 = 3

Before you go on to the next unit, look carefully at your keyboard. Are there any other extra characters that you haven't learnt to type? If so, mark them on your chart, and practise typing them.

Unit 58   Taking copies

When you're using your typewriter, you'll often find that you want to keep a copy of something you type. If you're writing an important letter, or if you're sending a report to your local paper, it's a good idea to keep a copy of what you've sent: partly because if there's an argument afterwards about whether you really said you'd pay that extra rent it's useful if you have an exact copy of what you did say; and partly because things *do* get lost in the post.

If you want to make one or two copies of what you're typing, the simplest way is to use carbon paper. Take out your carbon paper. If it's not in a box, try to find one to keep it in. If it gets creased it will produce very messy carbon copies.

Carbon paper is coated on one side. To make a copy, you:

1. Lay your backing sheet face upwards on your table.
2. Lay a sheet of typing paper on the backing sheet.
3. Lay a sheet of carbon paper, coated side downwards, on top of it.
4. Lay another sheet of paper (right side uppermost) on top of this.
5. Pick up all three sheets together and insert them into your typewriter so that the coated side of the carbon is facing the roller.

Then type in the usual way. You can make more than one carbon copy in this way – on most typewriters you can make up to six. All you have to do is to add another layer of paper and another sheet of carbon for each extra copy you want.

If you prefer it, you can make copies by using NCR paper. You can buy this from the stationer's. It comes in sets with full instructions. With it you can make copies without having to use carbon paper; but it is more expensive.

Using a photocopier is another method of making copies. Many big stores and some railway stations have them. You put a coin in the slot to get your copies. Again, this is much more expensive than using carbon paper; but it's a quick and accurate way of making copies of anything.

Lastly, in many big towns there are "instant print" shops. If you're the secretary of a club or society, these can be very useful. If you have to send a circular to all members, for example, you can type one letter and take it round to the instant print shop, which will run off, say, a hundred copies for you. They're fairly cheap, and will often print things while you wait.

Before you go on to your next unit, type out the numbered instructions for making carbon copies to keep in your folder. Take one carbon copy of it.

Unit 59   Using capital letters

You've already learnt how to type capital letters by using the shift key. In this unit, you're going to learn the occasions when capital letters are normally used.

You'll already know many of the rules. Refresh your memory though, by typing out the following. Set your margin stops at **30** and **80**, and your tabulator stop at **35**:

(1) A capital letter is typed at the beginning
of every sentence.

(2) A capital letter is used for the pronoun **I**.

(3) A capital letter is used at the beginning of
days of the week: **Monday**, **Tuesday**, and so on.

(4) A capital letter is also used at the beginning of the names of the months: **January**,
February, and so on.

(5) A capital letter is used at the beginning of
people's names - both forenames (or
Christian names) and surnames. It's used
for all proper names: towns, countries,
counties, all start with a capital letter.
When an adjective formed from a country's
name passes into common use, though, often
you stop using a capital letter. You'll
find that **french polish** is typed without
a capital letter; and so is **russian salad**.

(6) Perhaps because they're regarded as proper
names, nicknames are usually typed with an
initial capital letter. The **Iron Duke** and
The Little Emperor are examples of this.

(7) Names of societies are also typed with
initial capitals: **National Union of Jour-
nalists**, **Society for the Relief of Frost-
bitten Laplanders**, and so on.

(8) Names of the deity are typed with an
initial capital letter, and so are the
pronouns **His**, **Him**, **He** when they refer to
God. Many terms relating to the church
also take an initial capital - **Holy Com-
munion**, for example.

(9) Periods in history are sometimes typed with
an initial capital letter: **The Middle Ages**,
The Iron Age, **The Industrial Revolution**.

(10) Capital letters are used for many

abbreviations, especially when they con-
sist of only one letter to represent one
word: **J D Foresbry Esq OBE BA**. It's common practice - and much less work - to omit
the full stops after abbreviations like
this.

(11) Lastly, capital letters are often used for
headings. They give them greater empha-
sis.

Before you go on to your next unit, read through what you've typed.
It's a long exercise – but, then, you can type now!

Unit 60 Correcting your mistakes

However proud you are of your new-found skill as a typist, the fact
remains that you may occasionally (very occasionally!) make a mistake.
This unit is to show you how to put it right.

If your error consists of typing one letter instead of another, it's fairly
easy to put right, provided that you spot the mistake while the paper is
still in the typewriter. There are two ways of doing this.

The first is to use a **chemical eraser**. There are two kinds: one to
correct the top copy, and one to correct carbon copies. To correct an
error while the paper is still in the typewriter, you put a piece of the
carbon corrector, treated side downwards, over the error on the carbon
copy. Then put a piece of top-copy corrector, treated side downwards,
over the error on the top copy. Then you type the **wrong** letter again.
The effect of the strips of correcting paper is to cover the error. When
you have re-typed the wrong letter, remove the strips and type the right
letter.

A second method is to rub out the error with a **typewriting rubber**.
Before you start using a rubber, remember that any impression on the
top copy makes an impression on the carbon copy as well. If you rub
out briskly on the top copy, you'll make smudge marks on the carbon
copy – unless you put a piece of paper beneath the carbon so that *it*
takes the smudges when you're rubbing out. So the procedure is:

1. Find error.
2. Put piece of paper behind carbon copy.

3. Rub out error on top copy.
4. Take out piece of paper from behind carbon.
5. Rub out error on carbon copy.
6. Type correct character.

If you find that it is difficult to rub out a letter without rubbing out adjoining characters as well, use an eraser shield. This is a small piece of tough celluloid punched with holes of varying sizes. You can put the celluloid over your typing, with a suitable-sized hole over the error, and rub away to your heart's content without rubbing out other letters at the same time.

Correcting errors is more difficult if you don't discover them until **after the paper has been taken out of the machine**. If this happens, pull the paper-release lever forward, and put the paper back into the typewriter. Rub out the wrong letter. Then, with the paper-release lever still forward, move the paper about until it is in exactly the right place for you to strike the new letter. This isn't easy. You have to get it exactly on the line horizontally, and exactly in the space provided vertically. However, apart from its use in correcting errors, doing this is good practice in getting to know your machine.

If you correct mistakes in this way, you have to **correct each carbon separately**. Because the impression made by carbon paper is different from the impression made by the ribbon on the top copy, you'll have to cut out a small piece of carbon paper and put that on the carbon copy before you type in the new letter.

If you make the mistake of leaving out a letter, you'll have to follow the same procedure, but you'll have to rub out two or three characters. In the gap, you type in the two or three letters you have rubbed out, plus the extra letter. To do this, move the roller to the first space. Then half depress the **backspacer**, and type in the first letter; then half depress the backspacer again, and type in the second letter; and so on. By working in this way, you should manage to squeeze in an extra letter.

Before you move on to the next unit, type this sentence:

If you want to be a good typist, you mst always
practice regularly.

Rub out the **mst**, and using the backspacer type in **must**. Then rub out the **c** of **practice**, and type in **s** to spell **practise**.

Then type the same sentence in its uncorrected form, and take the paper out of your typewriter. Then put it back in and correct the errors. Look at your work carefully. Can you detect the forgeries?

Unit 61 Typing a letter

Typing letters is for most people the most important thing about being able to type. In this unit, we're going to see how it's best done.

If you have headed paper you don't need to type your address at the top of the letter. If you haven't headed paper, you can type the address by centring each line on the paper. This takes quite a lot of time, though. A simple way of setting out your address is to set the tabulator key for the middle of the sheet of paper and to start each line at this point. Your address would then look something like this:

> **Flat 24**
> **Blinkton House**
> **578 High Street**
> **Blanktown**
> **Bilcestershire**
> **16A 2E1**

There's no need to type a comma after the street number, and there's no need to type a comma at the end of each line. What is very important is to **include the postcode** at the foot of the address. If you have a telephone number, the simplest place to type it is at the left-hand margin point, on a line with the first line of the address. This would then look like this:

Tel: 09–437 5860   **Flat 24**
                                   Blinkton House
                                   578 High Street
                                   Blanktown
                                   Bilcestershire
                                   16A 2E1

Your ref: 127/12   **1st January 1981**

Below the address, you leave at least two line spaces before you type the date. You can leave more if you're typing a short letter on a piece of quarto or A4 paper. There's no need, when you type the date, to put a comma after the name of the month, or to put a full stop at the end of the date, after the year.

If you want to type a reference, you type it at the left-hand margin point on a line with the date. For personal letters, this isn't usually necessary. But if you're writing, for example, about your insurance policy, you *should* quote the number of the policy on your letter. If you're writing to your landlord, you should quote any reference he has quoted previously, as it will help him to find the necessary file.

Three line spaces (or more if your letter is a short one) under the reference, you type the name and address of the person to whom you're writing. This may sound unnecessary as you're obviously going to include his name and address on the envelope – but it is important for any official letters. If you keep a copy of a letter you write, it helps you to see at a glance from your carbon copy the name of the person to whom you've written.

The name and address of the addressee are usually typed in single-line spacing. They might look like this:

J C Jones Esq
Messrs Jones & Long
423 Blanktown Road
Anderton
Bilcestershire
E2R LA6

You don't need to type commas at the end of lines – or full stops after the initials.

Notice in this example the use of the word **Messrs**. It's short for the French **Messieurs**, meaning roughly the plural of the English word **Mr**. So don't use it before:

1. An impersonal name, like The **XYZ Company**.
2. A title, like **Sir Alfred Briggs & Sons**.
3. A limited company. A limited company is a legal body, not a collection of **Mr's**.

Another three line spaces below (or more if your letter is a short one), under the name and address of the addressee, you type what is called the **salutation**. This may be **Dear Sir** if the letter is a formal one, or **Dear Fred** if you're just writing to a friend. There's no need to type a comma after it. Two line spaces under the salutation you type any heading that you want to put to your letter. You can also, if you prefer, put a reference like the insurance policy number here. So the next part of your letter would look like this:

Dear Sir

Policy No. 1745/86

An official letter would look something like the one on page 118.

But a personal letter would look however you wanted it to look; and might begin **Mike you beast** and end **Cheers! Jenny**.

Then follows the main part of your letter. There's no need to indent for the first lines of paragraphs, unless you prefer to do this. When you've finished your letter, you type at the left-hand margin point what is know as the   **complimentary close** – that is, **Yours faithfully** (if the letter is a formal one); **Yours sincerely** (if the letter is slightly less formal) or **Love from**, if you're just writing to a friend.

If you're writing an official letter, it's useful to type your name at the left-hand margin point, under your signature. It makes it easier for people to see at a glance who is writing the letter. It's also a good idea in official letters to type in a note at the foot if you're enclosing anything with the letter. If, for example, you're writing to your solicitor about a lease, you can type at the foot of your letter:

Enc: Photostat of lease

Example of typed letter

Tel: 09-437 5860

Flat 24
Blinkton House
578 High Street
Blanktown
Bilcestershire
16A 2EL

Your ref: 127/12

1st January 1981

J C Jones Esq
Messrs Jones & Long
423 Blanktown Road
Anderton
Bilcestershire
E2R LA6

Dear Sir

I am writing to draw your attention to the dangerous condition of the lift in Blinkton House. On two occasions recently, it has become jammed between floors, fortunately at times when it was empty. I am sure you will realize the danger of one of the tenant's being trapped in the lift, apart from the inconvenience caused when the lift is not in operation.

I should be grateful if you would arrange for the mechanism to be completely overhauled as a matter of extreme urgency.

Yours faithfully

David Brown

Unit 62   Typing envelopes

Whatever size envelope you use, the address should be typed parallel to the long edge of the envelope. And it should be typed so that there is a gap between the first line of the address and the top of the envelope of at least 1½ inches (37 mm). This is to leave room for the postmark.

The name and address are typed on the envelope in the same way as they are inside the letter, except that the name of the town is usually typed in capital letters:

J C Jones Esq
Messrs Jones & Long
423 Blanktown Road
ANDERTON
Bilcestershire
E2R LA6

If you have to type a large number of envelopes at a time, there are two ways of saving time when you type them.

The first is by **chain-feeding** them into your typewriter. You put the first envelope into the machine, and type the address on it. Then you put the second envelope behind the first at the back of the roller. Then, when you turn the roller to take the first envelope out, you'll automatically be bringing the second envelope into position for typing.

A second, and quicker, method is to use **perforated labels**. If you use a roll of labels, you can type the names and addresses one after the other in a continuous flow. After you have typed them all, you can separate them and stick them on the envelopes.

Perforated labels are also available in sheets. If you are likely to want to send out letters to the same people regularly, you can use sheets of perforated gummed labels, and take several carbon copies of them. Then, when you next have to send out, for example, a circular letter, the labels will be ready typed.

Before you go on to the next unit, practise **chain-feeding**. You can use this technique for typing index cards, as well as envelopes.

Unit 63   Looking after your typewriter

A typewriter, if you treat it with respect, lasts for years. Its lease of life can, however, be shortened drastically if it is maltreated.

First – **avoid damage**. If you have to lift your typewriter from one room to another, move the margin stops together so that the roller doesn't suddenly shift from one side to the other when you're carrying the machine. Carry it from the back, putting both hands firmly under the base. If you lift it from the front, you're much more likely to press against the keys and bend them.

Another way in which the keys are likely to get bent is if the typewriter is left on the floor. If you're going to keep a typewriter on the floor (and if you haven't much space it's often the only place when you're not using it), you must have a case to keep it in. Some typewriters are sold in cases. For others, a case can be improvised. A wooden box covered in Fablon placed over a typewriter on the floor will prevent damage – and will also mean that you aren't wasting floor space, as you can use the surface of the box as a coffee table.

Apart from the risk of damage to the typewriter, there's a very real risk of damage to you if the typewriter is left on the floor without a cover. It's easy, in an absent-minded moment, to step back on to it, and overbalance.

Keeping the typewriter clean is also important. If you're not using your machine, keep it covered – either in its own box or under a soft cover. This matters particularly if you live in an industrial area.

If you use a typewriter rubber to correct mistakes, try to move the roller before you rub out so that the dust from the rubber doesn't fall into the typewriter.

If the keys get dirty – and you can see this easily because the quality of your typewriting will be much less clear – clean them gently. You can buy a special cleaner – either in the form of a putty-like substance that you press on to the keys, or in the form of a strip on to which you type. Or you can use a brush to clean the keys. Make sure you rub the brush backwards in the direction of the keys – not across them. If you haven't a typewriter-cleaning brush, an old toothbrush (with any remnants of toothpaste removed!) will do admirably.

Dust from the surface of your typewriter can be removed easily with a duster. Dust from the inside of the machine is more difficult. A quick and easy way to do this if you have the right fitting is to use the small soft brush on the vacuum cleaner. The chief thing to avoid is any kind of harsh cleaning.

Another thing to avoid is oil. A typewriter kept covered and in a fairly normal room temperature shouldn't need to have oil poured into it to make it function efficiently. Far too many typists think that they can compensate for the amount of rubber dust that they have let fall into their typewriters by pouring in oil. The effect isn't to counteract the rubber dust: the oil merely makes the dust stick more! More typewriters are ruined by too much oil than by too little.

Occasionally, something really *does* go wrong with a typewriter. If this happens, there is only one answer: a mechanic. Almost any shop that sells typewriters will be able to arrange to have your typewriter serviced – either in your own home or on their premises. It's worth having any faults put right. I did once know a typist (and a full-time one at that) who for years used a nail file whenever she wanted to change her margin stops. It doesn't make for easy typing though. And that, after all, is what this book is all about.

Unit 64   Using your typewriter

Now you've learnt to type, what are you going to do with your new skill? Here are some suggestions.

Letters. Typing is much quicker than handwriting – and much easier to read! Typewritten personal letters are now accepted by almost everyone, although it's still a courtesy to write by hand "thank-you" letters and letters of condolence.

Apart from personal letters to friends, use your typewriter for all your business letters – and keep carbon copies of them. You'll need a file to keep the copies in – but you're already used to keeping things in a folder in the course of working your way through this book. If you're going to make the best use of your typewriter, you'll need a simple filing system so that you have somewhere safe to keep your papers.

In the home. A typewriter is a useful thing to have around the home. You can use it for all sorts of things. Typing labels for jars and tins and copying favourite recipes from friends are two examples.

Literary work. Anyone who has any sort of literary bent needs a typewriter. Armed with one, you can send pieces of news to your local paper, or write articles and send them off to editors. If you're going to do this, you need to keep to a few simple rules:

1. Use A4 paper of a good quality.
2. Type on one side of the paper only.
3. Leave wide margins.
4. Type in double-line spacing.

5. Use your backing sheet to make sure that all the pages contain the same number of lines.

6. Number the pages.

7. Send a stamped addressed envelope for the return of your typescript.

The work of the honorary secretary. If there's a club or organization in which you're interested, you may want to help with running it. A good typist is always in demand for this kind of work. It's essential that you work in a fairly orderly fashion, and keep carbon copies of all the letters you write.

Earning money. If you want to earn some extra money, you can use your typewriter to do this. Possible sources of work are:

1. Publishers do at times have authors' typescripts that have to be re-typed. Type out a letter and have it duplicated, and then send it to a selection of book publishers. You'll find names and addresses in *The Writers' and Artists' Year Book* (listed in the booklist).

2. If you're near a university, students' theses often have to be typed. Type out a card advertising the services you have to offer, and send it to the secretary of the students' union, asking her to put it on the noticeboard.

3. If you can add shorthand or PitmanScript to your skill, you can offer to take dictation and type people's letters. A useful book to help you teach yourself PitmanScript is *Take Note* (see the booklist).

4. An advertisement in the local paper may bring you work. An advertisement in one of the weeklies such as the *New Statesman* costs more, but will reach a wider readership.

5. Try writing to likely customers direct. If you live in a town where you know there's a freelance writer, type a letter to him asking him if he needs any further typing help. Other possibilities are university lecturers, local councillors, vicars and ministers.

Community action. You probably won't be paid anything for it – but a typewriter gives you a marvellous opportunity to make things happen: whether it's organizing a petition to get traffic lights at a dangerous crossing, or trying to save your town's last patch of green.

Booklist

A good dictionary is important for checking spelling and the meaning of words. *Chambers Twentieth Century Dictionary* (published by W & R Chambers Ltd) is a particularly good one.

As a general reference book, *Whitaker's Almanack* (published by Whitaker's each year) is probably the most comprehensive.

For help with dividing words at line-ends, *Collins Gem Dictionary of Spelling & Word Division* is valuable.

The Post Office Guide (yearly – to be bought from any large post office) is useful if you send out a lot of letters and packages.

For literary work, *The Writers' and Artists' Year Book* gives details of magazines, book publishers, and the law as it affects writers. It's published each year by A & C Black.

And, if you want to teach yourself some form of shorthand, there is *Take Note in PitmanScript* by Colin Allan, published by Pitman.

Appendix

BITTELWASH COMMUNITY ASSOCIATION

NOTICE

Notice is hereby given that the Annual General Meeting of Bittelwash Community Association will be held at All Saints Hall, Bittelwash, on Wednesday, 31st January, 19--, at 8 pm.

Nominations have been received for the following offices:-

Chairman	Herbert Rowden
Secretary	Myra Gann
	Stephen Kemp
Treasurer	Angela Collar
Committee Members	Fred Gann
(six vacancies)	Elizabeth Kemp
	Anne Murdoch
	Jane Naylor
	Frank Nugent
	Patricia Nugent
	John Rowden
	Charles Turner
	Anthony Wallace
	James Wallace

The following **motions** have been proposed:-

1. That Mr David Rowden be made a life member of the Association in recognition of his services to the village

2. That the secretary should be instructed to apply for the registration of the Association as a Charity

Members are reminded that only those whose subscriptions were fully paid as at 1st December, 19--, are eligible to attend the meeting and to cast votes in the election of officers and committee members.

BITTELWASH COMMUNITY ASSOCIATION

ANNUAL GENERAL MEETING

(To be held at All Saints Hall, Bittelwash, on Wednesday, 31st
January, 19--, at 8 pm)

AGENDA

1. Chairman's opening remarks

2. Apologies for absence

3. Appointment of tellers and scrutineers

4. Minutes of last Annual General Meeting

5. Annual reports from:-

   (a) Secretary
   (b) Treasurer

6. Election of officers and committee members

7. To consider the following motions:-

   (a) That Mr David Rowden be made a life member of the Association
       in recognition of his services to the village
   (b) That the secretary should be instructed to apply for the
       registration of the Association as a Charity

8. Any other business

BITTELWASH COMMUNITY ASSOCIATION

Minutes of a meeting held at All Saints Hall, Bittelwash, on
Wednesday, 28th March, 19--, at 8 pm

Present: Herbert Rowden (Chairman)
Myra Gann (Secretary)
Angela Collar (Treasurer)
and 98 members

Apologies for absence were received from Fred Gann, David Camburn,
and Jason Beer.

1. The minutes of the last meeting on Wednesday, 28th February,
19--, were read by the secretary and signed by the chairman as
being a correct record of the proceedings.

2. Matters Arising

   (a) Myra Gann reported that a meeting had been fixed for 22nd
   April, when the committee would meet the members of the Rail
   Travellers Association to discuss the possibility of joint
   action over the proposed cutdown in rail services.

   (b) Angela Collar reported that the Association had now received
   the cheque for one hundred pounds from the trustees of
   Bittelwash Charities.

3. Bittelwash Redevelopment Scheme

Alan Rowden gave a talk, illustrated by slides and maps, of the
proposed scheme for the redevelopment of the centre of Bittelwash.
A vote of thanks was proposed by Julia Goldfinch.

4. Any Other Business

The chairman reminded members that the annual ceremony of the
blessing of the boats would take place on the east beach on
Sunday, 15th April, 19--.

5. Date of Next Meeting

The date of the next meeting was fixed for Wednesday, 25th April,
19--. It would be held as usual in All Saints Hall at 8 pm.